Jaime J. Sucher

Shetland Sheepdogs

Everything About Selection, Care,
Nutrition, Behavior, and Training

BARRON'S

CONTENTS

2

WHAT IS A SHETLAND SHEEPDOG?

Dogs are considered the first domesticated animals. The actual domestication process is hard to trace because it is impossible for archeologists to distinguish tame wolves from early domestic dogs. They will agree, however, that the earliest indisputable records of "dog" remains date back more than 12,000 years.

Humans and Dogs

Long ago, our ancestors learned how to domesticate wolves and as a result, this wonderful creature that we call "dog" has become a part of our culture. At first, dogs were valued as hunters; as time went on, their immense loyalty made them valued protectors of human life, property, flocks, and herds. While in modern time we may still use them as hunters, herders, and protectors, our relationship with dogs has gone well beyond that of owner and worker. Dogs have become our dearest companions and our favorite pets.

Origins and Early History

Although the Shetland Sheepdog clearly has older roots, the first clear records of its existence date back to the early 1800s. At about this time, visitors to the Shetland Islands

brought back to the mainland of England and Scotland small farm dogs called toonies. These toonies that were being used to care for sheep in the Shetlands were described as a small breed of Collie. By using this description, little doubt exists that the toonies were what we now call Shetland Sheepdogs, or Shelties.

Today's Sheltie directly descends from the small sheepherding dog used in the northern islands of Scotland. The harsh climate and rough terrain of the islands do not make them the ideal location to raise an abundance of large cattle. Vegetation is sparse on these islands, and there are few places to hide from the severe North Sea storms that frequent the island. With limited food sources and space requirements, it would be almost impossible for large species of cattle, or any other large land animal, to survive a long time in the Shetlands.

Luckily, nature has a way of solving its own

problems. In order for animals to survive in the Shetland Islands, they had to be adaptable. Smaller, hardier animals could survive in this harsh environment; they require less food and can find shelter in many more places than larger animals can. So, after generation upon generation of evolution, literally all of the animals common to the Shetland Islands have become smaller and hardier than their cousins on the mainland. This reduction in size can be seen in both the domestic and wild animals that inhabit the islands. Besides the Shetland Sheepdog, one of the best known examples of this is the Shetland pony. Like the diminutiveness of the Sheltie, the small size of the Shetland pony is very much a result of the islands' environment.

The rugged landscape and severe weather of the islands rule out commercial farming, while the isolated location of the Shetlands makes them an impractical place to establish many factories. For a long time, the raising of livestock has logically been the major industry of the Shetland Islands.

The types of livestock that can be effectively raised on the Shetland Islands must be able to adapt to the terrain and climate. After generations of being raised on the islands, the domestic cattle and sheep evolved into miniature versions of their mainland predecessors.

While the exact origins of the Shetland Sheepdog are unknown, it is generally believed that this breed descended from a small working dog that was also the progenitor of the modern Collie. Accentuating the effects of the island environment is the fact that the small working dog was also crossed with other small breeds believed to have been residing in, or indigenous to, the islands.

How long the evolution of the modern-day Shetland Sheepdog took to complete is not known, for no written records exist. Because these dogs were bred in the relative isolation of the islands, it took a long time before the breed became known to dog enthusiasts of the outside world. Thus, it was not until 1909 that the Sheltie obtained its initial recognition by the English Kennel Club when it was classified as a Shetland Collie. In 1914, the breed obtained a separate classification and has since been known as the Shetland Sheepdog. In 1915, the first Challenge Certificate was awarded to the breed.

Over the years, several Shetland Sheepdog clubs have been formed. Unfortunately, their history has always been one of controversy over variations in the acceptable size and type of the breed. The oldest club, the Shetland Sheepdog Club of the Islands, was founded in 1908. Their standard asked for a "rough Collie in miniature" with a height not to exceed 15 inches (38 cm). The Scottish Shetland Sheepdog Club, founded in 1909, at first requested "an ordinary Collie in miniature" with an ideal height of 12 inches (30 cm). Later, this club changed its standard to "a modern show Collie in miniature" and changed the dog's ideal height to 13.5 inches (34 cm). The English Shetland Sheepdog Club, an offshoot of the Scottish club, was founded in 1914. Like its parent club, its members also had their own opinion as to the ideal Sheltie. The English Club called for "approximately a show Collie in miniature" with an ideal height of 12 inches (30 cm). This was later changed to an acceptable range of 12 to 15 inches (30–38 cm), the ideal being 13.5 inches (34 cm). Adding to the controversy was the British Breeders Association, an offspring of the English club. They called for "a show Collie in miniature" while maintaining the same heights as their parent club.

Finally in 1930, both the Scottish and English clubs revised their standards to read "should resemble a Collie (rough) in miniature." Even today, some variations still exist among the different clubs in the British Isles; however, these differences are now in a much more refined form.

The different standards among the various clubs reflected the breeders' struggle to obtain and perpetuate the ideal size and type. As mentioned, the progenitor working Collie was bred with other smaller breeds to reduce its size. The crossbreeding risked introducing characteristics that were contradictory to the true Collie type. Crossbreeding the working Collie with the small Spaniels, for instance, resulted in undesirable traits such as wavy coats, hound-like ears, long bodies, large round eyes, and wagging tails. On the other hand, these Spaniels also brought the beneficial characteristic of calm and devoted dispositions. It is also believed that a little yellow dog from Iceland that had a dark muzzle and pricked ears influenced the breed.

To counteract the undesirable traits that were beginning to appear, crosses with modern Collies were made. This cross was responsible for improving the head properties, such as ear type and expression, as well as enabling the breeder to obtain the beautiful, weather-resistant coat. However, even this crossbreeding had its faults, such as legginess, excessive size, loss of substance, and imbalance.

Thus, breeders had to breed these new smaller Collies in such a way as to produce a dog having all the traits associated with a correct Collie. At the same time, they attempted to keep the correct balance and size that we associate with our modern-day Sheltie.

The Shetland Sheepdog Standard presently approved by the Kennel Club of Great Britain has essentially the same requirements set forth by the American Kennel Club (AKC). If you plan to register your Sheltie in England or show your dog internationally, obtaining a copy of the British Standard would be wise.

The major difference between the standards of the Kennel Club of Great Britain and the AKC lies once again in the Sheltie's height. The British standard states that the ideal height for Shelties is 14.5 inches (37 cm) for males and 14 inches (35.5 cm) for females. The AKC standard calls for a height of between 13 and 16 inches (32.5–40 cm) at the shoulder. Any height measurement over one inch (2.5 cm) above the ideal is to be considered a serious fault.

Shelties in America

While records exist of the Sheltie being brought to New York in 1911, it was not until 1929 that the American Shetland Sheepdog Association (ASSA) formed. When developing the Shetland Sheepdog standard for AKC approval, the ASSA combined the best of all the British standards. As stated, the current AKC approved standard specifies a height from 13 to 16 inches (32.5–40 cm).

The first Sheltie breeders in the United States encountered problems like those in the British Isles. In their attempts to improve the physical characteristics of the breed, the American Shelties were crossed with their larger cousins, the show Collie. In order to maintain the small size associated with the Sheltie, crosses with only smaller Collies were made. However, as in Great Britain, this practice resulted in oversized dogs.

Since then, improvement of the Shetland Sheepdog has been done only through selective breeding. Now the common practice is to breed Shelties that have some weaker traits with dogs of the same breed that are stronger in the targeted physical or behavioral characteristics. As a result, the modern show Shetland Sheepdog has become a beautifully balanced dog that has the type, weather-resistant coat, and expression of a Collie combined with the Sheltie's smaller size, character, and charm.

Characteristics of the Breed

The following descriptions are an interpretation of the AKC-approved Shetland Sheepdog Standard. The Standard is a complete written description of the breed; it includes how it should look, act, and move. You can obtain a copy of the written Standard from the ASSA or the AKC.

General Appearance: Shetland Sheepdogs are small, alert, rough-coated, long-haired working dogs. They must be sound, agile, and sturdy. The outline should be so symmetrical that no part appears out of proportion to the whole. Males should look masculine, while females should look feminine.

Size: The Shetland Sheepdog should measure between 13 and 16 inches (32.5–40 cm) at the shoulder when the dog is standing naturally. The measurement is taken from the ground directly up the foreleg to the top of the shoulder blades.

Coat: Because the Sheltie was originally bred as a herding dog for the harsh climate of the Shetland Islands, his coat must be suited for the weather. Shelties have a double coat. The outer coat consists of long, straight, coarse hair. The undercoat is short and furry. The combination of these two coats gives the Sheltie his full standoff quality. The hair on the Sheltie's face, feet, and tips of the ears should be smooth. The mane of the Sheltie should be thick and full.

Because males should look more masculine, their mane and frills should be more abundant than those of a female. The hair on the forelegs and hind legs is feathered, with the hind legs heavier than the forelegs on top but smooth below the hock joint (the joint equivalent to a backward knee). The hair on a Sheltie's tail should also be thick and abundant.

Color: There are wide variations of color in shelties. Black, blue merle, and sable (ranging from golden to mahogany) marked with white and/or tan are all recognized color variations. (Blue merle consists of mottling of bluish gray color on the face and back.) Unacceptable color

variations include rustiness in a black or blue coat, faded colors, conspicuous white spots, or more than 50 percent white.

Temperament: The Shetland Sheepdog should exhibit the temperament of a herding dog. This breed is intensely loyal, affectionate, and responsive to its owner or handler, but they may be "reserved toward strangers." However, dogs of this breed should show no signs of fear or cringing.

Head: The head, when viewed from the top, should "be a long, blunt wedge tapering slightly from ears to nose." The nose is always black. The top of the skull is flat, without a prominent skull cap. The cheeks of the Sheltie are flat and should smoothly curve into a "well-rounded muzzle." The muzzle should be the same length as the skull, with the balance point at the inner corner of the eye when viewed from the side. The flattened line along the top of the Sheltie's skull should be parallel to the flat top of the muzzle but on a higher plane due to the "pres-

ence of a slight but definite stop." The under-jaw should be deep and well developed. It is rounded at the chin and extends to the base of the nostril. A Sheltie's jaw is clean and power-ful. When his lips are tight, the upper and lower lips meet and create a smooth seal all the way around. The teeth should be level and evenly spaced, with the dog having a scissor bite.

Eyes: A Sheltie's eyes are medium in size and have dark, almond-shaped rims. The eyes must be dark. (Blue eyes are permissible only in blue merles.) The eyes are set at a slight angle to the skull.

Ears: This breed has small and supple ears with the tips breaking forward. The ears are located high on the skull and are carried about three-quarters erect. When resting, the Sheltie will fold his ears lengthwise and throw them back into the frill.

Expression: The basic shape and contour of the head, along with the location and position-ing of its eyes and ears, all combine to produce

the Sheltie's expression. Under normal conditions, the expression should be "alert, gentle, intelligent, and questioning." In the presence of a stranger, the expression should be one of watchfulness and caution; however, no sign of fear should appear.

Neck: Shelties have a muscular neck that should be arched and long enough to carry his head proudly.

Body: The body should appear moderately long from the shoulder to the rump, while the back is level and well-muscled. A Shetland Sheepdog has a deep chest with the brisket (lower chest) reaching to the back point of the elbow. The ribs should be well-sprung but flattened at the lower half; this allows for the free movement of the foreleg and shoulder. The abdomen of the Sheltie should be tucked

up fairly well even though his coat may give the abdomen an appearance of being flat or rounded.

Forequarters: When starting at the withers (the highest point of the shoulder), the shoulder blade should slope downward and forward at a 45-degree angle to the shoulder joints. At the very top of the shoulders, the withers are separated by only the vertebrae. However, they should slope outward at an angle sufficient to allow for the spring of the ribs. The upper arm should join the shoulder blade at a 90-degree angle. The elbow joint should be located midway between the withers and the ground. When viewed from any angle, the forelegs of the Sheltie must appear straight, muscular, clean, and strong-boned. The pasterns (back of the foreleg) should appear strong and flexible.

Feet (front and hind): The feet are oval with well-arched toes that fit tightly together. Shelties have deep, tough pads and hard, strong nails on their feet.

Hindquarters: There should be a slight arch at the loins. The croup (highest point of the rump) should gradually slope to the rear. The hip bone should be set at a 30-degree angle to the spine. The Sheltie should possess a broad and muscular thigh. The thighbone should be set into the pelvis at a right angle (this corresponds to the angle made by the shoulder blade and the upper arms of the forelegs). The stifle bones (which join the hind leg and the body) should be "distinctly angled at the stifle joint." The overall length of the stifle bones should be equal to or slightly longer than the thighbone. The hock joint (the next joint below the stifle) should be angular and sinewy with good, strong bones and ligaments. The hock should be short and, like the foreleg, should be straight when viewed from all angles. Dewclaws should be removed.

Tail: The tail should be long enough that when it is laid along the back edge of the hind legs, the last vertebra will touch the hock joint. When the tail is at rest, it should be carried straight down or at a slight upward curve. When alert, the Sheltie will normally lift his tail. However, the tail should not curve forward and over his back.

Gait: When trotting, the Shetland Sheepdog should give one the impression of "effortless speed and smoothness." The proper trot will show no signs of jerkiness, stiffness, or up-and-down motion. The rear legs should appear to be the driving force. The line on which he runs must be straight and true. If all the angulation, musculature, and ligaments are correct, the rear legs of the trotting Sheltie will reach well under his body and then retract smoothly, propelling the dog forward. Proper reach of stride of the forelegs also depends on the proper angulation, musculature, and ligaments of the forequarters; however, it can only be achieved if the dog has the correct width of chest and construction of the rib cage. When trotting, the front feet should be lifted only enough to clear the ground when the legs swing forward. When viewing the dog from the front, both the forelegs and hind legs should be perpendicular to the ground when the dog is walking. When trotting, the legs should become angled inward. When running swiftly, the feet are brought inward, toward the center line of the body. When moving, the Sheltie should not cross his feet or throw his weight from side to side.

SHOULD YOU BUY A SHELTIE?

As a herding dog, the Shetland Sheepdog has some traits that make it an ideal "family" dog. Likewise, their diminutive size allows them to adapt to living in a city apartment as easily as living on the farm.

Making an Intelligent Choice

As the name implies, the Shetland Sheepdog was originally bred to tend sheep. In order to be successful in this endeavor, the Sheltie had to be loyal, obedient, and courageous. A sheepdog had to protect his flock from danger yet not frighten the herd itself. In addition, the sheepdog had to be hardy, independent, and able to protect himself from his harsh surroundings. The Shetland Sheepdog was bred to achieve the temperament needed for the job, and his thick coat gives ample protection from the weather. Through years of selective breeding, these traits have become synonymous with the breed and can be found in all of today's Shelties.

Shetland Sheepdogs make excellent house pets. They are fast learners and extremely obedient. They are small, easy to care for, and beautiful. They possess the perfect temperament to be with children and are equally suited to be a watchdog. All these traits make the Shetland Sheepdog the ideal pet for a diverse range of people regardless of their living space or their age.

Whether to buy a Sheltie is an important decision. Lack of awareness of the responsibility of dog ownership can result in an unhappy relationship for both the dog and the owner.

Free-ranging dogs constitute a major problem in the United States as well as in many other countries. Studies indicate that this problem is due more to human irresponsibility than to a dog following his wild instincts. In the long run, the situation can lead to the outbreak of diseases from nonvaccinated, homeless animals. These facts emphasize the importance of responsible pet ownership.

After considering all the points, if you still wish to purchase a Sheltie, find out if a chapter of the American Shetland Sheepdog Association is in your area. Its members can help answer your relevant questions.

Male or Female?

Once you have decided to buy a Shetland Sheepdog, you will have to choose either a male or female dog. In this breed, little difference exists between the sexes. Both have about the same disposition and are of equal physical proportions. As with most breeds of dogs, the males are usually more likely to roam while the females tend to stay near home. The only time you might prefer a specific sex is if you are interested in breeding the dog.

Regardless of whether you select a male or female, if you have no intention of breeding, have the dog neutered or spayed. Because an alarming number of dogs in the United States are homeless, owners should take all possible precautions against the increase of unwanted animals. Spaying the female dog also avoids the messiness that will occur when she is in heat. A spayed female will be more likely to avoid breast tumors, ovarian cysts, false pregnancies, and other ailments. Neutering a male dog virtually eliminates the chance of testicular or prostate cancer.

One important thing to consider before spaying your dog is that spayed or neutered dogs may not compete in any purebred conformation shows and some obedience trials. There are, however, some obedience trials where spayed dogs may compete, as well as a large variety of other activities including frisbee, flyball, and freestyle dance competitions, to name a few. If you and your dog plan on getting involved in a showing or competing in field, agility, herding, or any other competition, you can learn more about them through the ASSA or by going online before you have your pet neutered.

Adult or Puppy?

While the choice of gender in a Sheltie may not be important, whether you buy an adult or puppy certainly is. When making this choice, keep the following in mind.

One of the greatest rewards of owning a Shetland Sheepdog is watching him grow from an unbelievably cute, awkward, tiny bundle of fur into a beautiful, dignified, loyal adult. However, this requires a great deal of patience, time, and energy. A properly trained adult results from diligent attention by owners who gave their puppy understanding, love, and the needed thorough training. All too easily dog owners neglect their duties. The result is a relationship in which neither the dog nor the owner is happy.

For the person who does not have the time to devote to a puppy, selecting an adult Sheltie offers other advantages. A well-trained Shetland Sheepdog makes a fine pet. Mature Shelties will usually have little trouble adapting to a new household, thereby saving the new owners the time needed to raise, train, and housetrain a puppy. An adult Sheltie, by needing significantly less attention than a puppy, makes an ideal pet for the elderly or for a working family. The greatest drawback to buying an older Sheltie is that you may find correcting bad habits the dog may have already acquired to be extremely difficult.

If you are interested in obtaining an adult Sheltie, start by contacting a reputable breeder. It may be possible for you to buy or even adopt

CHECKLIST

Considerations

1. Do you have the time, energy, and patience to raise a dog properly?
2. If you purchase a Sheltie puppy, would you be willing to change your schedule to meet the dog's needs? Puppies are not independent and require frequent feedings and closer supervision.
3. Are you willing to devote some of your free time to the dog? Do you travel on weekends or take long vacations? Are you willing to travel only to areas where you can bring your Shetland Sheepdog? Although dogs can withstand the stress of travel fairly well, they are prohibited in many hotels and motels.
4. Do you understand the long-term commitment involved in owning a Shetland Sheepdog? A Sheltie may live a dozen years or more.
5. Do you have a yard, or is a park or wooded area available where your dog can get his much-needed exercise? The Shetland Sheepdog is a small breed and can be comfortably housed even in a small apartment. However, Shelties are a working breed. Both their physical and mental welfare depend on getting sufficient exercise.
6. Finally, can you afford to keep a Shetland sheepdog? Aside from the initial expenses of buying the dog and necessary supplies, feeding may cost as much as $40 per month. Additional expenses include annual visits to the veterinarian.

Rescue Organizations

Consider working with a Shetland Sheepdog rescue organization. These nonprofit groups are dedicated to finding people who can provide a caring, loving home to abandoned, abused, or unwanted dogs. Rescue groups can be found on the Internet or through the ASSA.

These organizations are a great source of information and will provide sound advice before, during, and after an adoption. They will also make sure that the dogs they put up for adoption are up-to-date on vaccinations and are spayed (if old enough). Rescue groups are committed to finding the right match for their dogs, so you have a better chance of getting a dog that is right for your lifestyle. As these organizations are not always privy to a dog's history, they take extra time to understand a dog's temperament and match him to prospective owners. In this way they spend more time finding the right home for their dogs and less going through the rescue process for a second time.

a dog that is too old to be bred safely. By doing this, you can be sure of acquiring a Sheltie raised by a caring and knowledgeable person.

When choosing between a Sheltie puppy and an adult, keep in mind that raising a puppy will allow you to train him to the habits of your household. Adult dogs, on the other hand, need significantly less attention, which means less work, especially for an older owner.

If you are looking for a show dog, you have two options. First, you can purchase a potential show puppy from a reputable breeder and raise him yourself. This way you will have the satisfaction of knowing that you have done the job yourself. Alternatively, you can purchase a mature show dog. This way, you are assured of your Sheltie's quality and beauty.

Purchasing Your Sheltie

The first step in purchasing a puppy is to contact the secretary of the ASSA or the AKC. Get from them a list of reputable dealers and well-established, registered Sheltie breeders in your area. Visit as many breeders in your area as possible.

I strongly recommend that you avoid purchasing a puppy from the Internet before seeing him in person. While the Internet is a great way to get important information that you may need, it has also become a tool for scam artists to make a lucrative business fleecing unwary consumers using misrepresentative photographs. This is not to say that you should not purchase from a reputable breeder that advertises on the Internet, but you should make every effort to visit those breeders in your area to be sure that the information they place on their Web sites is legitimate. Also keep in mind that while it may be more convenient to obtain a Sheltie from a local breeder, traveling the extra distance to visit as many breeders as possible can sometimes pay dividends.

Visit each kennel to inspect the dogs and conditions in which they are kept. The time and effort you spend in finding the right Sheltie will save you trouble and heartache later on.

When visiting the kennels, keep in mind that the quality of your puppy will directly reflect the quality of the breeder. Conscientious breeders will make every effort to satisfy you in order to maintain their reputation. Always feel free to ask the breeder questions, regardless of how silly they may seem. A good breeder will be able to answer all your relevant questions and be of invaluable help in selecting your puppy.

Place the least emphasis on the price of the puppy. Never be swayed into buying a dog because he is cheap. The old adage, "You get what you pay for," is all too true when buying a dog. A bargain price may indicate the dog was raised strictly for profit by an inexperienced breeder or that the dog is in poor health. A more expensive dog from an experienced breeder may save you a lot of future veterinarian bills.

You should also avoid Shelties from kennels not dedicated solely to breeding and raising Shetland Sheepdogs. Breeders who raise several breeds of dogs are not always knowledgeable about the special needs of each breed.

As you visit each kennel on your list, pay special attention to the dogs' housing. Be sure the surroundings are clean and that the dogs have room to move about freely. Observe the coat conditions and overall appearance of all of the dogs. Each of these factors indicates the quality of the operation. Once you have found a dealer or breeder in whom you have confidence, you must then choose your puppy.

Choosing Your Puppy

Examine the puppy's coat; it should be smooth and shiny. His eyes should be bright and the puppy should be sturdily built. Shetland Sheepdog puppies should look alert and be slightly cautious, for they are herding dogs. In most cases, avoiding both hyperactive and overly sedate dogs would be best.

If you watch the puppies play together, you get an idea of their individual temperaments. Some may be bolder, others more shy. The puppy's temperament is a good indicator of what the dog's adult behavior will be like. You can therefore select a dog whose disposition will fit in your home life. I have found that dogs that tend to be a little more quiet and sedate make ideal pets for homes whose occupants lead a more quiet life style, whereas the bolder puppies are better suited for families that have active children (or parents) where the dog will not get too overwhelmed by lots of noise and activity.

Another good indicator of the puppy's temperament is his mother's behavior. After all, the puppy inherits many of his behavioral characteristics from his sire (father) or dam (mother). Observe how the mother reacts to people. She should show no signs of fear and only the slightest amount of misgiving at the most.

As herding dogs, Shelties are inherently protective. The dam may take a little time before she senses that you, a stranger, mean her and her litter no harm. This type of behavior is actually desirable in a watchdog. However, the dam should show no sign of aggression.

If the puppy appears to be in good health and of sound temperament, the next step is to check his pedigree papers. These papers are a written record of the dog's recent ancestry—a dog's family tree. All the show champions in his lineage will be marked as such. Ask if the dog's medical history is in the Canine Health Information Center (CHIC) database. CHIC is jointly sponsored by the AKC and the Orthopedic Foundation for Animals (OFA). Its goal is to provide a source of information for owners, breeders, and scientists to assist in the breeding of healthy dogs. The CHIC database for Shelties presently includes results of eye clearance tests by the Canine Eye Registry Foundation (CERF); it also includes the results of OFA and other veterinary orthopedic group tests for hip dysplasia, von Willebrand disease (a form of hemophilia), and the multi-drug sensitivity (MDR1) DNA test. Optional testing that may be included in the CHIC database include autoimmune thyroiditis, Collie eye anomaly DNA test, elbow dysplasia (OFA), congenital cardiac disease, and American temperament testing (test results registered with the OFA). If the breeder does have his or her dogs listed, the results can be reviewed online at *www.caninehealthinfo. org*. If the breeder does not have his or her dogs' test results in the database, you should certainly ask why.

If the dog's pedigree is satisfactory, ask for the date the puppy was wormed. Be sure to get a written record of this to show your

A dog requires annual immunizations against all infectious diseases as well as an annual heartworm test. Puppies and adult dogs may also have to be wormed. If you do not plan to breed your Sheltie, spaying or neutering is recommended. This will cost from $75 to $150. If your dog should get sick or injured, he may need additional, sometimes costly, medical attention.

Finally, you will have to pay an annual licensing fee to your county or city. You will have to pay a fee to register your dog with the AKC as well as annual dues if you join the ASSA.

The long-term expenses of owning a Shetland Sheepdog are much greater than the purchase price. Therefore, carefully consider these costs before you decide to buy a dog.

veterinarian. Do not be afraid to ask questions. A reputable breeder is as concerned with the puppy's welfare as you are. Also, do not be offended if a breeder asks questions about your experience with dogs and where you plan to raise your puppy. Take this as a sign of concern. In addition, keep an open line of communication so that the breeder can help you with any future problems.

Expenses

Though the initial purchase price of a Shetland Sheepdog varies, expect to spend at least $400. Potential show dogs may sell for $1,500 or more. Generally, a younger puppy will be less expensive than an older dog, because less time and money will have been invested in him.

Food may cost as much as $30 or $40 a month. You must also purchase equipment for feeding, grooming, and housing your dog.

Bringing Your Puppy Home

Once you have selected the best puppy for you, you will have to arrange to take him home. The puppy should be seven weeks old when he moves to his new home. A puppy of this age should adapt very easily to his new environment but not be old enough to have picked up many bad habits. Recent studies have shown that during their eighth week, puppies become especially sensitive to environmental changes. If you cannot pick up the puppy during the seventh week, wait until the ninth week. Rather than risk creating behavior problems, wait until the puppy is ready for change.

If you select a Sheltie puppy from a local breeder, visit your puppy several times before bringing him home. This will allow your puppy to get used to you and can help alleviate some of the stress that a newly separated puppy experiences.

HOUSING AND SUPPLIES

The Sheltie does not require large amounts of room indoors; however, it is important to their mental and physical health that they have a protected feeding and sleeping area, where they can eat and rest in peace and have access to outdoor areas to get plenty of exercise.

Indoor Requirements

I have previously mentioned that the diminutive size of the Shetland Sheepdog offers many advantages when it comes to indoor space requirements. Logic dictates that a smaller dog requires a smaller space, and in this case, that is true. However, dogs are territorial animals. Although a Sheltie's territory does not need to be very large, it must not be too small.

A Shetland Sheepdog, whether an adult or a puppy, requires a quiet living area where he can feel comfortable and secure. Inside your home, you must provide your dog with a territory of his own—his regular eating and sleeping areas. In locating these areas, keep in mind that once established, these areas should not be moved. The dog will feel secure and protected only if he has a quiet, reliable place to rest undisturbed. This area should neither isolate the dog nor subject him to heavy human traffic.

Good resting areas are in corners where the dog is protected on two sides. These areas should also be draft-free and not in direct sun-

light. The area should also make confining the dog's movements easy when you go to bed or when you leave the house. Of equal importance is that the Sheltie's sleeping area be at the right temperature. A puppy requires the temperature to be between 70 and 75°F (21–24°C). This range is warm enough to minimize environmental stress that can lead to upper respiratory infections, and is not so warm as to make the dog sensitive to outside cold.

A Sheltie's sleeping area may be equipped with either a sleeping box and pad or a crate with a pad. Make this choice in advance, depending on your method of housetraining. (See the chapter, Basic and Advanced Training, page 75). I recommend using a crate. It can also be invaluable for transporting and disciplining your puppy. Dogs are instinctively den animals, so the confined space will make a puppy feel safer and more comfortable than would an open sleeping box.

The crate should be approximately 24 inches (61 cm) high by 24 inches (61 cm) wide by 30

inches (76 cm) long. It must have strong welds that cannot be broken by an active puppy. Fiberglass shipping crates are a good choice because they are lightweight and easy to clean.

The crate will be your puppy's house when you are not around to supervise. Some crates can also be used to carry your puppy when you go for a drive or to the veterinarian

If you decide not to use a crate, purchase a sleeping box. Make sure it is large enough to accommodate a full-grown, spread-out dog. Line the box with shredded newspapers. Then place an old blanket over this layer. Your dog will find this very comfortable for sleeping.

If you are purchasing a sleeping box, avoid those made of wicker or other soft wood materials. An active puppy can easily chew apart these types of beds. Likewise, if you decide to build your own box, use only non-splintering hardwoods. Because many stains and paints are toxic, leave the box unfinished.

When you are bringing home an unhouse-trained puppy, do not give him an expensive pad. Puppies have little control over their bladder or bowels, so anything used in their bed should be either disposable or washable. In addition, be sure that anything you put into the bed is clean. Puppies are very susceptible to ailments because their immune system is not fully developed, and their resistance to disease is low.

Like his sleeping place, a dog's feeding place should never be changed. Changes in sleeping and feeding places can cause your pet unnecessary stress. An animal under stress may exhibit behavioral changes as well as changes in many biological functions, including problems with digestion and excretion. Placing your dog's feeding area into an easily cleaned room, such as the kitchen, is best.

Outdoor Requirements

Unlike most toy and miniature breeds, the Shetland Sheepdog is a rugged breed and may be kept outdoors—in most climates—all year round. However, bringing your Sheltie indoors on cold winter nights is advisable.

If you decide your dog is to live outdoors or if you leave your dog outside when you are not home, you must provide him with a fenced enclosure or run. The run should be at least 6 feet (2 m) wide by 15 feet (5 m) long by 6 feet (2 m) high. It should be constructed of strong chain-link fence. You can place partially buried boards around the bottom to prevent the dog from digging under the fence. The run can be as large as your yard. However, it should not be smaller than the size stated.

Use a few inches of smooth pea gravel as a base. This will provide drainage when it rains and prevent the dog from becoming muddy.

Do not use concrete as a floor, because concrete will retain the smell of urine. The run must also provide your dog with some shade and shelter.

The best form of outdoor shelter is a doghouse. Whether you build your own or buy one, make sure it is raised several inches off the ground to avoid dampness and insects. The doghouse must be properly constructed to protect the dog against wind, rain, and cold, for even a minor draft can lead to serious respiratory ailments. The doghouse should be approximately 36 inches (91 cm) long, 30 inches (76 cm) high, and 30 inches (76 cm) wide. If the house is too small, the dog will not be able to stand or sleep comfortably. However, do not make the house too large. During cold weather, the dog's body will provide the only form of heat. For this reason, insulting the structure is also best.

Keeping your Sheltie's house as clean as possible is important. When constructing a doghouse, you can do several things to make cleaning easier. First, by hinging the roof, you can easily fold back the top of the doghouse to make the inside easily accessible. Next, you can line the floor of the structure with an easy-to-clean, waterproof material such as linoleum. Over that you can place an old blanket. If you use cedar planks or plywood in the construction of the doghouse, you can get the added benefit of having the natural oils in that wood help repel fleas.

To prevent the inside of the house from being exposed to the cold winter winds, you should place the front opening so that it faces south. If you hang a piece of canvas or a blanket over the opening, making sure it overlaps sufficiently, you can help eliminate drafts. If you live in a climate where winter nights become very cold, you should find a place indoors where your dog can sleep. You may also consider purchasing a doghouse for your beloved pet. There are several good ones available, and I recommend the fiberglass "igloo" style, which has the protective qualities your dog needs and are easy to clean and sanitize.

Additional Accessories

The first days after you bring your new puppy home are bound to be very busy and exciting. To avoid additional work or confusion, purchase the following items in advance, and keep them available.

The most important pieces of equipment, at least from your growing Sheltie's point of view, are the food and water dishes. Both food and water dishes should be nonbreakable,

heavy, and sturdy enough so that a Sheltie with a voracious appetite cannot tip them over. Stainless steel and ceramic are both suitable materials. If you choose to use a ceramic bowl, however, be sure it was not fired with a lead-based glaze. Using bowls covered with these glazes, over a long period of time, can cause lead poisoning. Plastic bowls should not be used because they may leach chemicals into a dog's drinking water, which can be harmful to his health.

During the life of your Sheltie, purchasing more than one collar may or may not be necessary. Your puppy will require a light collar but not necessarily a strong one. I recommend using either a leather or nylon collar that is adjustable to fit both a Sheltie puppy and an adult. Bear in mind, though, that these collars deteriorate with age and would therefore need to be replaced eventually. If your Sheltie is an adult, you may choose to use a chain collar, but be sure it is not too heavy or bulky for your dog. Another type of collar that you may want to purchase is a training collar, which can come in very handy when it is time to teach your dog the basic commands.

Leashes come in a wide variety of lengths and materials. You may want to purchase more than one type. For regular walks, use a leash that is only a few feet long. This will enable you to bring the dog to your side quickly, should the need arise. It will also prevent your Sheltie from taking a destructive stroll through your neighbor's perfectly manicured garden. If you are lucky enough to possess a large yard, a 30-foot (10-m) leash with an automatic reel is useful. Because a Sheltie is not a large, strong dog, you do not need to get a leash made of anything stronger than leather or nylon. This is doubly true of Sheltie puppies. Sheltie puppies will chew, or attempt to chew, on anything that passes in front of their noses. Therefore, you should never purchase a chain leash for your puppy. Chewing on the chain can damage a puppy's teeth.

While collars and ID tags are essential, microchips and tattoos are becoming more popular because they can't fall off and can be of great help in recovering your pet should he become lost. Microchip capsules are about the same size as a grain of rice and can be implanted under the pet's skin, usually between the shoulder blades. The owner then sends the information to a registering agency along with a current contact and alternate contact. When a pet is found, any agency with a scanner, including many animal care and control agencies, veterinary clinics, and research labs, can quickly identify a code that links the animal to its owner through a national database. Tattooing involves placing a permanent ID code on the

T I P

Reflective Tape and ID Tags

I recommend using reflective tape (or tags) on both the collar and leash. These will make both you and your dog more visible to car drivers, making your nighttime walks much safer. You should also attach an identity tag to your dog's collar that gives your name, address, and telephone number. This inexpensive tag could prove invaluable should your beloved pet ever become lost.

necessary if your dog becomes seriously hurt and has to be taken to a veterinarian. A dog in severe pain may react unpredictably, so be prepared. When buying a muzzle, get one that can be adjusted for size. Remember that the head of a Sheltie puppy and that of an adult dog are very different.

Tweezers and rubbing alcohol should also be on hand. Use tweezers to remove ticks properly and rubbing alcohol to disinfect the wound.

Dog Toys

As with children, toys are an essential part of a dog's life and are important to both his physical and mental well-being. Toys signify playtime. They let your puppy know that there is more to life than training sessions, eating, and sleeping. Playing with toys gives a dog exercise and allows a dog to work out frustration that he may be experiencing. In addition, toys allow a puppy to develop his survival instincts. If you watch your Sheltie playing with his toys, you will see this for yourself. Watch your puppy get low to the ground and attempt to creep up on his target. Observe him studying his opponent, waiting until the time is right. Then watch him pounce and render his prey harmless. This entire act may take all of five seconds, but it is part of every puppy's instincts to survive. If all this is not enough to convince you of the importance of toys, I will give you one last reason to use them. Giving your puppy toys will spare your furniture, clothing, and other valued possessions from small, but well-defined, teeth marks.

From the time a puppy begins to teethe, he should always have a chewable toy on which to gnaw. Rawhide bones are excellent chew toys. They become soft enough to not harm a young

skin of the dog. The tattoo is usually placed in the pet's ear, abdomen, or on the inside of the pet's thigh. The finder of the lost pet can call a national database that uses the code to obtain the owner's current address and phone number. With both these systems you must remember to update all contact information if you move or change phone numbers (the same goes for your pet's ID tag). Some tattoos can fade over the years, so make sure they are visible. Since microchips can move, you can ask your vet to check its location and functionality during your dog's routine examinations.

The owners of Shetland Sheepdogs rarely need a muzzle for their dogs. However, you should keep one readily available just in case. If you are planning on taking your Sheltie abroad, note that some foreign countries require all dogs to wear muzzles. A muzzle may also be puppy's teeth and, at the same time, will help strengthen your Sheltie's jaw muscles. Since a Sheltie puppy can quickly reduce a small rawhide bone to almost nothing, make sure to replace the bone before it becomes small enough for the puppy to swallow whole. Avoid giving your dog any toy that he can shred and swallow, for this can cause choking or blockage of the digestive tract.

When choosing toys for your Sheltie, make sure they are designed for small dogs and are made of 100 percent nontoxic materials. Some forms of plastic are toxic, and many forms of wood can splinter. To be on the safe side, never give your Sheltie any painted items. Some older types of paint contain lead, which may be harmful if swallowed in excess. Varnished toys are also potentially toxic and should be avoided.

Not all your Sheltie's toys need be store bought. Some of the best times my dogs have ever had were when we played hide and seek with some big cardboard boxes. Tennis balls are also among their favorite toys. If you decide to use a ball from around your house, it should be of the proper size and material. Do not use golf balls or Ping-Pong balls, because they can be chewed on and swallowed. Do not be afraid to use your imagination. You can use many simple household items to keep your puppy entertained for hours.

Just remember to be selective in the items you give your puppy for toys. A Sheltie puppy will chew almost anything that will fit into his mouth. In addition, a mischievous Sheltie will tend to seek out anything with your scent, such as your old shoes and clothing. For this reason, keep these items out of your puppy's reach. Also, never give your puppy either your old slippers or toys that resemble valuable objects. A sheltie puppy does not know the difference between an old slipper and your new one. This is true of anything of value to you.

CARING FOR YOUR SHELTIE

It is inevitable that your first days home with your new puppy will be rather hectic, but some careful planning can help reduce the worry and stress that both you and your companion will experience.

Necessary Preparations

Before you bring your new puppy home, be sure to purchase all the necessary equipment and accessories, such as food and water dishes, collars, leashes, grooming supplies, and so on. In addition, you should also choose the puppy's food (as recommended by the breeder) and purchase an adequate supply of it.

When you have bought all the supplies and have placed them in readily accessible locations, begin to puppy-proof your home. Remember that a young puppy is very curious. As he roams through your house, he will sniff, paw at, and chew almost everything. For this reason, place all potential hazards out of the puppy's reach.

Remove all poisons, including paints, cleaners, disinfectants, insecticides, and antifreeze. Store them in an area inaccessible to your puppy. Also, remove all sharp objects such as nails and staples. If you have an older home, make sure your dog does not eat paint chips containing lead.

Electric wires must also be moved out of your puppy's reach. A dog chewing on electric wires can be injured or killed by the resulting shock.

Finally, you should decide where the Sheltie's feeding and sleeping areas will be, and equip them accordingly. By doing all of these things, you can make the upcoming transition period much easier for both you and your puppy.

Adjustment

During those first few days in his new home your puppy will undoubtedly be stressed, as he will find himself being taken away from the familiarity and security of his mother and siblings and find himself in an unfamiliar world that is full of strange new sights and sounds. To reduce the stress you will want to make the transition period go as smoothly as possible; let your puppy know he is entering a calm, safe, and secure home, and plan on making your puppy's first few days at home as quiet as possible.

When your puppy arrives, he will probably want to urinate or defecate. Instead of entering your house, walk the puppy to a place you have chosen for his elimination area. Give the

CHECKLIST

Puppy Safety Rules

Before bringing your Sheltie puppy home, review these seven rules with your family and friends. In addition to preventing injury, these rules will help your puppy to feel comfortable and safe in his new home and increase his confidence in you and your family.

1. Avoid unnecessary excitement. New owners have a tendency to invite over everyone they know to see the new member of their family. Young visitors will usually run around screaming with excitement. Let the puppy adjust to his new surroundings in peace before subjecting him to numerous strangers.

2. Prohibit rough play. Puppies are very fragile creatures and should be handled with care. Avoid overhandling. Make sure the children do not poke the puppy, pull his ears, or subject him to any other rough handling.

3. Be sure everyone in your household knows the proper way to lift and carry your puppy (see page 31 for technique). If any visitors desire to pick up the puppy, instruct them how to do so.

4. Avoid picking up the puppy too much. Allow him to do his own walking whenever possible. This will provide some exercise and improve the puppy's motor skills and physical abilities.

5. Do not give bones or other hard objects to a young puppy. Until a puppy reaches about six months of age, he has only his milk teeth and cannot chew hard objects.

6. Do not subject your puppy to unnecessary heights. Avoid placing him onto tables, counters, or beds, because a fall could be disastrous. When placing the puppy onto an elevated surface, such as a grooming table, someone must be present the entire time to assure the puppy's safety.

7. Try never to leave the puppy unsupervised during the first few weeks.

puppy about ten minutes to relieve himself, and then praise and pet him for doing so. This will help the puppy learn to defecate and urinate outdoors.

To help the puppy adjust, let him sniff around your home undisturbed. Then help him learn the location of his food and water dishes. Let your puppy continue to roam about, but do feel free to pet him and play with him. When he tires, pick him up and put him into his sleep-

ing box or crate. Within a few days, the puppy should learn where his sleeping area is and when tired, find his bed on his own.

To me, the next step in training your puppy is the hardest test you will face. Furthermore, it is your first test. Failure here will mean greater problems in the future. Your puppy will probably whine, whimper, and wail because he is in an unfamiliar place and because he misses his mother and siblings. However, you must remain firm. If the puppy sleeps in a crate, do not let him out. If you do, he will wail every time he wants to leave the crate. If you use a sleeping box, you might try to reassure the puppy by speaking softly, but do not take him from the box. Your puppy must learn to deal with loneliness as soon as possible.

If you must leave the house during your puppy's first few days, be sure he is not left alone. If no family member is available, ask a neighbor or a close friend to puppy-sit. An unsupervised, curious puppy means only one thing—a mess.

Soon after your puppy arrives, you must begin to train him. Training will require time, energy, patience, understanding, and of course, love. From the minute your Sheltie arrives, begin to teach him his name; then you can move on to the other basic commands included later in this book.

Handling a Sheltie

Everyone in your family must learn how to lift and carry your puppy. Improper handling can pain and possibly injure the dog. Place one hand under the puppy's chest, and support the rear and hind legs with the other hand. Never pick up the puppy by placing only one hand under his abdomen. Never pick him up by the scruff of the neck. Both of these methods can hurt the puppy.

A healthy, adult Sheltie will weigh only 14 to 16 pounds (6.4-7.7 kg), so most people can lift him in the same fashion as a puppy. I do urge you to pick up and carry an adult dog only when necessary. If your Sheltie can jump over an obstacle or climb up a flight of stairs to his destination, then let him. A herding dog needs a lot of exercise.

TIP

Feeding

1. At first, keep the puppy on the same diet he was receiving from the breeder to minimize digestive system stress. If you want to change the puppy's diet, do it gradually by mixing in larger amounts of the new food while reducing the old food proportionately.
2. Try to feed your puppy on the same schedule as the breeder; however, if that is inconvenient, gradually shift the feeding times to meet your schedule.
3. From the start, try removing your puppy's food from him (while he is eating) for a few minutes, and then return it to him to continue eating. If you do this regularly, it will reinforce your position as "Master" over your dog (which is critical to successful dog training).
4. Never surprise your dog while he is eating (or sleeping). A surprised dog may act unpredictably, so be sure to explain this rule to everyone else in your household as well.

When moving an injured dog, take special precautions. If possible, wait for an experienced person to lift and carry the dog. If you must do this yourself, first place a muzzle onto the dog. A dog in pain may act unpredictably and snap at anyone who tries to help him. Then place one arm between the dog's forepaws. The hand on this arm should support the dog's midsection while the forearm should support the

dog's head. Use the other hand to support the dog's rear and hind legs. Do not allow the dog's midsection to sag or his head to fall forward. (For further information on treating a sick dog, consult the Ailments and Illnesses chapter, page 47.)

Shelties and Children

The Shetland Sheepdog is a herding breed. When he is with children, many of his inbred personality traits become even more evident. Shelties are loyal dogs and are full of pep and spirit. They will joyfully play with children while, at the same time, be alert for any signs of danger. This breed is rarely the aggressor in any confrontation. However, if any member of his family were attacked, the Sheltie would defend that person with a ferocity that belies his small size. Shelties are small, but they are quick to think and maneuver. In addition, their self-assurance and ruggedness make them formidable opponents, even to very large dogs.

A special bond will form between a Sheltie and the children in his family. Many years of hard life on the Shetland Islands have impressed upon this breed the need to cling to one family, be loyal, and obey its commands.

Although the Sheltie is a hardy and rugged breed, their small bodies will not stand up to all the abuse that many children can dish out. Even the most loyal Shelties may turn and nip at a child (or adult) he feels is deliberately trying to hurt him. All animals, including humans, have this instinctive defensive reaction. Children should be taught not to pinch and pull on the dog's hair, tail, or ears and always to avoid going near the dog's eyes. Children should be taught never to disturb a Sheltie while he is eating or sleeping. Explain that although the dog is a loving pet, he may nip at them if surprised or frightened. Also, teach your children how to meet a strange dog. They should not go to the dog but, instead, let him approach them. They should not move suddenly, and they should keep their hands below the dog's head. If the dog sniffs their hands and is still friendly, the children can pet him.

You can help assure an enduring relationship between your children and your Sheltie by involving them in the responsibilities of dog care. Encourage your children to help feed, groom, and walk your dog.

Shelties and the New Baby

Reports of attacks on infants by family dogs lead many people to get rid of their devoted pets when they have a new baby. This is truly a shame, for Shelties are at their best when they have children—including infants—to love. If you have or are planning to have a baby, take heart. Animal behavior experts who have studied this problem thoroughly have concluded that most dogs will not be aggressive toward a baby. They also believe, however, that dogs that tend to chase and kill small animals, or those that are aggressive toward people in general, should never be left unsupervised with an infant.

You should take several precautions to assure your Sheltie's acceptance of your new baby. Before the baby's birth, train your dog to sit or lie down and stay still in those positions for long periods of time. As you increase the length of time the dog remains still, accustom him to other activities occurring around him at the same time. Reward your dog if he stays still and does not attempt to follow you.

Once training is complete, simulate the other activities that will occur after the baby arrives. Use a doll to imitate carrying, feeding, changing, and bathing the newborn.

After the birth of the infant, give the dog something the baby used in the hospital in order for him to sniff, smell, and become accustomed to the baby's scent. Upon returning home from the hospital, allow the mother to greet the dog without the baby. Then place the baby into the nursery, and deny the dog access by using a screen door or folding gate. In this way, the dog can see and hear the infant and get used to his presence before dog and baby actually meet.

When you finally introduce the dog and baby, one person should control and reward the dog while another person holds the baby. Have the dog sit, and then show him to the baby. Keep them together for as long as the dog remains calm. For the next week or two, gradually increase the length of the dog's visit.

Never allow your dog to wander unsupervised in the presence of an infant. However, be sure to allow your dog to be present during activities that involve your newborn. Do not let the dog feel neglected because of the infant. The more activities in which you allow the dog to participate, the stronger the bond will be between Sheltie and child.

Shelties and Other Pets

Shetland Sheepdogs should get along well with other pets. Your Sheltie will rarely show signs of jealousy as long as he receives sufficient attention. If the pets substantially differ in size, such as with birds, hamsters, gerbils, and so on, not allowing these animals to play freely with your Sheltie is best.

If you own two Shelties, you will rarely have any problems. In fact, the dogs will probably enjoy each other's companionship. Many members of the herding breeds work in tandem with other dogs, and the Sheltie is no exception. You must remember, however, not to give the older dog any less attention than previously. Show the older dog that you care for him as much as always; then leave the two to establish their own relationship. You should have little difficulty getting the two dogs to live in harmony. In fact, if you show no favoritism to either dog, the older one should adopt and protect the younger one.

Before buying a second dog, however, remember that you will need additional equipment, including separate sleeping boxes or crates and food dishes. Also be sure you have the extra time, space, and money that a second dog requires.

Canine Social Behavior

If you plan to own more than one Sheltie, or if you wish to understand why dogs react as they do to humans and to each other, you must examine the dog's instinctive nature. Canine social behavior is similar to that of wild wolves. Wolves are pack hunting animals and require companionship of other wolves. This is also true for Shelties, though for domestic dogs, humans can also satisfy their need for company. Because of this need, you can punish a dog by isolating him during training sessions. In addition, as pack animals, dogs develop among themselves a dominant-subordinate relationship. In this relationship the "alpha" dog rules, and the rest of the pack will find their place in line (and during the training of your dog you will need to need to let him know that you are the "alpha"). This relationship allows a stable existence between dogs. Thus, if one of your dogs tends to be more dominant than another, do not worry. This occurs naturally and will prevent fights between dogs for food, living space, and human attention. This social ranking is largely determined by size, age, strength, and sex. This social dominance also allows a dog to obey his owner. During training, a dog learns that he is subordinate to the human members of the household.

Both dogs and wolves mark their frequently traveled paths or territory by urinating, defecating, and scratching the ground. In addition to such a boundary marking, females secrete a scent that signals their being in heat.

Female Dogs

If you own a female Shetland Sheepdog, you must take special precautions regarding pregnancy. A Sheltie female normally comes into estrus (in heat or in season) twice a year. Estrus is the period during which the female accepts mating with the male. This period usually lasts four to fourteen days. If you choose not to breed your female, you can take several measures to prevent pregnancy. As stated earlier, if you plan never to breed the female, have her spayed. The benefits are numerous.

Spaying your female dog will prevent her from roaming away from your home when she is in season. Also, it is the only sure way to prevent an unwanted litter. Finally, an unspayed female may suffer many ailments that a spayed dog can avoid. These include false pregnancies, uterine infections, ovarian cysts, and many types of tumors that attack the reproductive system.

Because spaying a dog is permanent, you must be positive that you will never want to breed your female. If you are at all in doubt, do not have your dog spayed. As your female gets older, you may wish to continue the line of the dog you have grown to love over the years. You can attempt to do this by breeding your female with another purebred male Sheltie. You cannot do this with a spayed dog. If you decide not to spay, there are other ways to avoid pregnancy in your female dog.

The most obvious way is to keep your female away from all the male dogs. This may not be as easy as it sounds. You would be amazed at the distances a male dog will travel to find a female in heat. In addition, stray male dogs may camp outside your house, waiting for you to drop your guard. For this reason, you must never let your female go outside alone during estrus. Even if you have a fenced-in yard, she would not be safe. To get at a female in heat, male dogs can perform supercanine feats.

During her season, your female will also undergo some attitude changes. The mating urge is very great at this time. Your female may be less obedient to your commands, especially if a male is nearby. So always walk your female on a leash when she is in heat, or you may end up running after her as she ignores your pleas for her to return.

For a female to discharge small amounts of blood during her season is perfectly natural. To prevent staining your rugs or furniture, you may wish to confine her to an easy-to-clean room. Sanitary napkins and diapers are also available for dogs in heat.

Boarding Your Sheltie

During the course of your lives together, almost inevitably you and your Sheltie will have to spend a prolonged period away from each other. You may be suddenly called away from home or have to go on a business trip, or maybe you need a vacation. If you live alone or if the members of your family are going to join you, you must arrange to have someone look after your dog.

Having a dependable neighbor whom the dog knows and trusts and whom you can instruct about your Sheltie's eating, playing, and walking routine is ideal. In this way, your dog will be able to stay in his familiar environment, your home. Unfortunately, things do not always work out this easily. Another great alternative is to keep your Sheltie at home and hire a pet sitter to check in on your dog throughout the day. You can check your phone book or the Internet for a professional pet sitter near you, or ask your veterinarian or friends for referrals.

If you must board your Sheltie, start by contacting the breeder from whom you purchased him. If the breeder is willing to care for your dog, you can be assured of expert care for a Shetland Sheepdog. If this is not possible, you may decide to place the dog into a boarding kennel.

Before you leave your Sheltie at a boarding kennel, I recommend that you inspect the facilities thoroughly. Make sure that the sleeping areas and runs are clean and that the operating staff at the kennel are knowledgeable. If all the conditions at the boarding facility are suitable to you, there need be little worry about your dog. A mature Shetland Sheepdog will have

little problem adjusting to this new environment. If it can be avoided, however, you should never leave a puppy younger than six months old, either alone or at a boarding kennel, for a long period of time.

Vacation Time

Vacationing with your Sheltie can be fun for both of you, but it takes planning. Not all airlines, cruise ships, and trains accept dogs, and many have significant restrictions, so you need to do your research. For example, some airlines will transport dogs only when the temperatures are not too cold or too hot, at both the place of departure and place of destination, and some will let dogs travel only in the cargo hold and not in the passenger cabin; so be sure to read all the rules on the carrier's Web site.

In the United States federal law requires that dogs traveling by air must be certified by a veterinarian within 10 days of the flight to be healthy, vaccinated, and free from contagious diseases. You may also have to deal with security. When you check in your baggage, you will also need to check in your dog. To do this you will need to remove the dog from his travel crate, which is put onto a conveyor belt and put through the X-ray check, while your dog walks with you through the metal detectors (so be sure to remove any metal ID tags).

If you decide to vacation in a foreign country, obtaining from the appropriate consulate a copy of the country's law pertaining to dogs is advisable. While most countries have minimal regulations about dogs, some do require quarantine. Some countries have laws about the use of muzzles. Most countries do require that your dog be immunized against the major

infectious diseases. You will need a valid health certificate from a licensed veterinarian. If you should require veterinary service while you are abroad, you can get helpful information from the American consulate or embassy.

Traveling by car can be the most fun for your dog. Many Shelties actually seem to enjoy car travel and will spend hours watching the passing scenery. When traveling by automobile, do not allow your pet to have free run of the car. You should confine your Sheltie to either his crate or the back seat. Open the window enough to give him some fresh air, but do not expose him to a draft. Drafts can cause eye, ear, and throat problems. Make rest stops at least every two hours, and allow the dog to walk and relieve himself. Keep him on a leash so that he will not run away. The inside of a car can get very hot, so allow your dog to drink regularly.

Never leave your dog unattended in a closed vehicle, particularly in the summer. If you must leave the car for a short time, designate a family member who will know what to do to stay with the dog and make sure the inside of the car does not get too hot.

Many young dogs may get carsick if they are not used to traveling. As a precaution, you can obtain motion sickness tablets from your veterinarian.

Once you have made all your traveling arrangements, it is time to pack. Your sheepdog suitcase should contain the following: food and water dishes, collar, leash, brush, blanket (and crate), and muzzle. Bringing enough canned or dry food to last the entire trip is advisable. If you normally feed your Sheltie fresh foods, accustom him to canned or dry food for a few weeks before your departure.

HOW-TO: GROOMING

Your Sheltie will need a thorough brushing every day and periodic grooming to maintain his coat in prime condition. Start handling and grooming your puppy as soon as possible so he will become accustomed to the procedure.

Equipment

Every Sheltie owner should have the following supplies: a comb, a slicker brush, a stiff-bristle brush, scissors, nail clippers, tweezers, ear-cleaning solution, and cotton swabs. Because the Sheltie is a relatively small dog and grooming him is easier when the dog is at table level, you may also want to consider purchasing a grooming table. No matter how experienced

you become at grooming your Sheltie, you should always have a small bottle of styptic powder in case of accidents that result in bleeding.

Daily Brushing

Start by using the stiff-bristle brush, followed by a slicker brush on the dog's back and sides, avoiding all the areas of the body with longer hair. By using the bristle brush first, you can untangle snarls before removing any shedding undercoat with the slicker brush. Use the stiff-bristle brush on the feathered hair on the legs, abdomen, chest, and tail. Once brushing is complete, use a comb to remove all loose hairs. If the feathered hairs of your Sheltie become

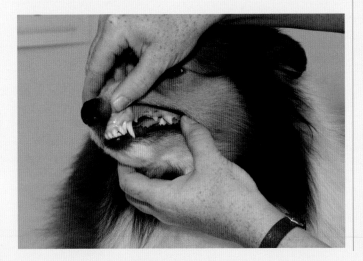

too long, you can trim them using sharp scissors. When brushing your Sheltie, you should look for signs of flea infestations. If you notice any other skin condition, seek the advice of your veterinarian.

Tipping the Ears

The shape of a Sheltie's ears may vary somewhat, resulting in differences as to how they should be groomed. When a Sheltie assumes an attentive position, his ears should stand semi-erect, with just the tips folding forward. Unfortunately, most Shelties need assistance to obtain this look. If your Sheltie has low, hound-like ears, you can trim off all the excess hair around the tips in order to reduce the weight that pulls them down. If your dog does have bent tips, then you may want to weight (or tape) them down. Consult with a breeder, veterinarian, or groomer about the best weighting procedure.

Ear and Eye Care

To avoid infections, trim all excess hair from the ear canals. A pair of tweezers helps remove any loose hairs that have gotten into the ear. Carefully remove any wax buildup using a commercial ear-cleaning solution. To clean the ear, hold it open with one hand, and gently clean inside the outer ear with a cotton ball dipped into cleaning solution. Use a fresh cotton ball for each ear. You can clean the outermost portions of the ear canal using a cotton swab that has been dipped into the solution.

Inspect your Sheltie's eyes regularly as well. Be sure they are clear and free of any discharge. You can clean around your dog's eyes with a moistened cotton ball to remove any dirt. Again, use a fresh cotton ball for each eye. If you notice any damage or inflammation, contact your veterinarian for advice.

Caution: Before cleaning your dog's eyes and ears for the first time, consult with your veterinarian to learn the proper methods.

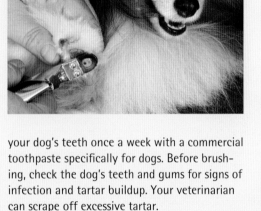

Nail and Paw Care

Check the bottoms of the dog's paws, and trim the hair between the paws as short as possible. This will improve the dog's traction and reduce the chance of infection in wet weather. Before you trim your dog's nails, learn how to use a pair of clippers. An experienced groomer or veterinarian can show you how to use them.

The center of the dog's nail is called the quick and contains the blood vessels and nerve endings. If you cut the quick, you will cause the dog much pain. Always cut the nail as close to the quick as possible, and be sure to hold your pet's paw firmly but gently. Be sure to have the styptic powder on hand.

Tooth Care

Tooth care begins with feeding your Sheltie plenty of hard foods to prevent the buildup of tartar. Excessive tartar can lead to deteriorating gums and tooth loss. You should also brush your dog's teeth once a week with a commercial toothpaste specifically for dogs. Before brushing, check the dog's teeth and gums for signs of infection and tartar buildup. Your veterinarian can scrape off excessive tartar.

Bathing

Bathing should be thought of as a last resort. Shampooing your Sheltie can remove the natural oils that weatherproof the coat. Excessive bathing also tends to dry out your Sheltie's skin and promote excessive shedding. Try to clean your dog with a wet, slightly soapy cloth.

When bathing is necessary, use a shampoo formulated for dogs. Be sure to rinse out all of the shampoo, which may irritate the dog's skin. Dry your Sheltie by rubbing him briskly with a towel. (You can also use a blow dryer.) Once most of the water has been removed, brush and comb out the coat. Keep your dog indoors and away from drafts while he dries.

WHAT DO I FEED MY DOG?

The nutritional requirements of dogs have probably not changed very much from the time they were first domesticated. Our understanding of those needs, however, has increased greatly in recent years.

The National Research Council (NRC), a division of the National Academy of Science of the United States, has interpreted vast quantities of data and published a study entitled "The Nutritional Requirements of Dogs." This study establishes the minimum amount of every nutrient (protein, fat, carbohydrates, vitamins, minerals, and trace elements) needed to maintain the health of the average middle-aged and older dog, as well as growing puppies.

The NRC study serves as a guideline for all companies that manufacture commercial dog food in the United States to help them formulate their products. In fact, for a dog food to be certified as "complete and balanced" in the United States, it must meet or exceed all of the nutritional requirements established by the NRC. In addition, it must also pass actual feeding tests that were established by the Association of American Feed Control Officials (AAFCO).

While their ancestors (wolves) are scientifically classified as carnivores, modern domestic dogs have evolved to a point where they can effectively utilize a wide variety of foods to meet their nutritional needs and are therefore considered omnivores. This allows modern commercial dog food manufacturers to use a wide variety of ingredients to achieve the mandated nutritional profiles. Unfortunately for the consumer, it can make it very hard to determine which dog food is best. To help decide what is best for your Sheltie, seek the advice of your breeder and veterinarian. Breeders will know what food works best on their Shelties, while veterinarians have a working knowledge of dog foods based on the experiences of other clients. A veterinarian will also be able to recommend a special diet should your pet's health dictate the need for one.

I strongly urge all dog owners to use a high-quality commercial dog food rather than preparing their pet's food from scratch. When preparing meals at home, it can be difficult to determine if you are giving your loving companion too much or too little of an essential nutrient. It is also significantly more expensive and much more time-consuming (time you can use playing and exercising with your beloved pet). If, however, you feel that as an act of love you want to prepare your dog's food from scratch, then I strongly advise you to read as many books as you can on animal nutrition and seek the advice of your veterinarian.

What Is High-Quality Dog Food?

Like human food recipes, the ingredients used to make commercial dog foods have varying degrees of nutritional value. While most "complete diets" are supplemented with a sufficient quantity of vitamins and minerals, the ingredients used in a high-quality dog food should be easily digestible and free of chemical

additives, which over the long term can have harmful effects on your pet.

When looking for a high-quality diet, check the label to make sure the pet food was tested using AAFCO procedures and is complete and balanced. This statement can be found at the end of the nutritional information panel.

Check the ingredients listing. By law, the label must contain a list of ingredients, with the most abundant ingredient (by percent weight) listed first and continue in descending order. The primary ingredients listed in a high-quality dog food should be easily recognizable, such as chicken, beef, lamb, brown rice, carrots, and peas. Ingredients such as cornmeal, wheat, soy, and white rice are carbohydrate fillers that are not easy to digest and provide little nutritional value. Be extra cautious with wheat- and soy-based products as they are both allergens. Look for foods that use meat meals, rather than animal "by-products." Meat meal is actually meat with the water removed, where "by-products" contain the indigestible parts of animals including feet, feathers, hooves, and hair. Finally, avoid foods that contain chemical antioxidants such as BHA and BHT. High-quality dog food will instead use vitamin C or vitamin E to prevent fats from turning rancid.

Feeding Table Scraps

Many people feel that they are obliged as loving pet owners to feed their precious pooches leftovers. Be warned that this practice has great potential for teaching your Sheltie really bad habits, such as begging. In addition, feeding the wrong table scraps to your dog can lead to obesity, which in turn can lead to health issues later on. I have also seen where this practice can lead to a dog refusing to eat his regular diet, which can also result in problems related to improper nutrition or malnutrition.

How Many Meals Do I Feed My Sheltie?

Relative to their body weight, Shelties can eat larger quantities of food than humans at a single meal, so they do not need to be fed as frequently. Adults can be fed one or two times a day. Puppies, however, need to be fed more often. A puppy between four weeks and three months old needs to be fed at least four times a day. Because dogs react well to routines, you should create a feeding schedule and stick with it. A good time to feed your dog is during the family meals, so he is occupied while the rest of the family is at the dinner table.

The Importance of Water

Of all the constituents in a dog's diet, there is none more important than water. Water is vital to every living cell and comprises nearly 60 percent of your dog's body weight. Unlike some animals, dogs cannot store much water and must constantly replenish whatever they lose. This means that you must make sure your dog has an adequate supply of water at all times. A Sheltie's water intake will depend on several factors, including air temperature, the type of food he eats, the amount of exercise he gets, and his temperament. Be sure to avoid giving your dog very cold water, especially after exercise or if he is showing signs of heatstroke. Cooling the dog's body down too fast can be counterproductive and can lead to other severe illnesses.

Does My Sheltie Need Nutritional Supplements?

This is a very controversial topic at the moment. While there is plenty of information available, it is often difficult to separate the information that comes from the manufacturers of nutritional supplements from that of independent researchers.

Naturally, the manufacturers of these items are interested in selling their products, but getting too much of some nutrients (such as vitamin D) can be toxic and have dangerous side effects. The amount of nutrients your Sheltie needs will depend on several factors, including diet, age, activity level, medical conditions, and environmental stresses. This means that not all dogs need nutritional supplements, while some

The Basic Nutrient Groups

Nutrient (Sources)	Nutritional Value and Symptoms of Deficiencies
Proteins (meat, eggs, fish, milk, soybean meal, brewer's yeast, wheat germ)	Provide amino acids essential for growth, development, and maintenance of strong bones and muscles; promote production of antibodies, enzymes, and hormones; deficiencies include poor growth, weight loss, loss of appetite, and poor hair and coat.
Fats (meat, vegetable oils)	Provide a source of energy and heat; supply essential fatty acids and fat-soluble vitamins (A, D, E, and K); make food more palatable; necessary for proper development of skin and coat; deficiencies include dry and coarse coat and skin lesions.
Carbohydrates (sugars, starches)	Help regulate energy balance; supply fiber and roughage to help regulate digestive system and help prevent diarrhea/constipation.
Vitamins (brewer's yeast, vegetables, fruits, cod liver oil, wheat germ oil)	Important in preventing numerous illnesses and diseases; help in regulating many bodily functions including growth and fertility.
Minerals/Trace Minerals (bones, meat, grains, fruit, vegetables)	Important in preventing numerous ailments and diseases; help in regulating many bodily functions including bone formation; help regulate water balance within a dog's body. (Trace minerals are so named because they are required in very small quantities.)

may have very specific needs. Before you give your dog any supplement, particularly vitamins or minerals, you should consult with your veterinarian. He or she will review with you the critical factors affecting your dog's nutritional requirements before giving you advice.

Special Considerations in Feeding Your Sheltie

While the NRC provides the minimum nutritional requirements for puppies and adult and older dogs, several other factors affect the type and quantity of food an individual dog needs. Growing puppies require about twice the amount of calories per pound of body weight as a middle-aged adult, while older dogs require about 20 percent less than an average adult.

As a result, puppies need special diets that are higher in proteins and fats to support their growth and metabolic needs, while older dogs, with their slower metabolism, can become overweight if their diet is not changed. Exercise and environment will also influence the quantity of food your Sheltie needs.

The best indicators that your companion is getting the proper amount of nutrition are his body weight and coat condition. Your dog is at an ideal weight if you can feel his ribs and can easily discern the waist from the ribs when running your hands down the side of his body. You should also be able to feel the abdomen slightly tucked up. If you have an underweight Sheltie, you will easily feel his ribs, vertebrae, and pelvic bones and you will not feel any fat on the bones. Severely malnourished dogs lose muscle mass, and puppies will have stunted growth. When a Sheltie is overweight, you cannot feel the ribs and you may see fat bulges over his back. In addition, the waist will not be discernable from the ribs and the abdomen will drop.

A dry coat and flaky skin may signify a fat, fatty acid, or vitamin deficiency. This condition is often accompanied by scratching and is often misdiagnosed by pet owners as external parasites or other skin ailments. The proper diet should produce a soft and shiny coat that is rich in color.

A Final Note on Feeding a Dog

You should know that dogs do not require a wide variety of foods and will not tire from

eating the same thing every day. If you feed your Sheltie a high-quality, well-balanced diet, he can thrive on that food for most of his life. If your dog is not eating properly, it may be an indicator of a physical or emotional problem. If your Sheltie falls off his diet for a day or two, there may not be any reason to worry and the dog's appetite may return on its own. But if your dog refuses to eat for more than two days, then it may be a sign of a serious problem and he should be taken to the veterinarian for an examination.

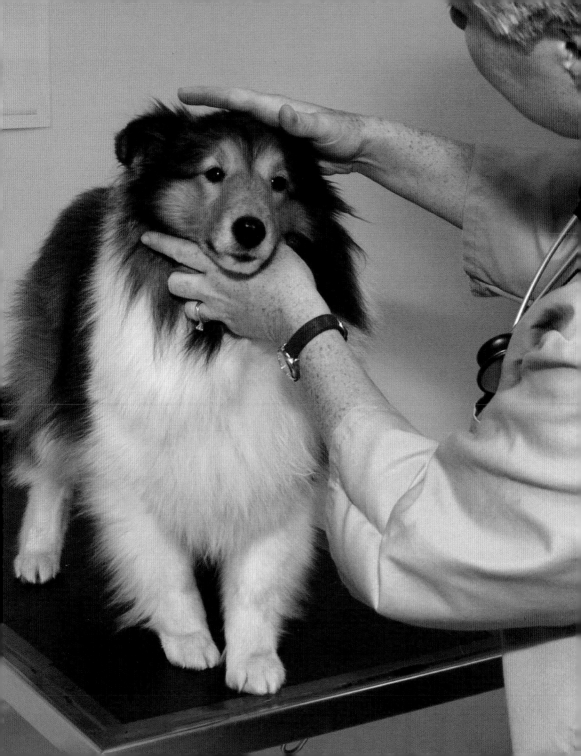

AILMENTS AND ILLNESSES

Dogs, like humans, are subject to a wide variety of illnesses. While the Sheltie is no exception, you will be glad to know that there are several things you can do to prevent many of the ailments described in this chapter.

Proper nutrition, good hygiene, and an adequate exercise program are essential in keeping your Sheltie healthy. By providing these requirements, combined with scheduled visits to the veterinarian, you can help your pet live a long and healthy life. You must never underestimate the importance of keeping scheduled appointments with your veterinarian. Early detection is the key to preventing many problems from getting out of hand, and it sometimes takes a trained medical eye to detect early symptoms.

Choosing a Veterinarian

The worst time to look for a veterinarian is when you really need one, so make sure you have chosen your veterinarian before you bring your new Sheltie home. When looking for a veterinarian, keep in mind that you are looking for more than a medical expert. You are looking for someone to meet the needs of both you and your pet—someone with "people" as well as "animal" skills.

Like your doctor, veterinarians often work with a staff of professionals (technicians, administrators, and aides), so you will likely want to evaluate the competence and compassion of the entire team. Location, fees, facility cleanliness, and suitability are also very important factors that you will need to evaluate. Weigh all of the issues that are important to you, but remember, you will probably be happier if you drive a few extra miles or pay a few extra dollars to get the care you want for your companion.

The best way to find a good veterinarian is to ask people who have the same approach to pet care that you have. Look for recommendations from friends, breeders, animal shelters, dog trainers, groomers, and/or pet sitters. Once you have narrowed your search, schedule a visit to meet the staff, tour the facility, and learn about the veterinary philosophy on treatment.

Once you feel you have completed your research, it is time to make your choice. Only you can determine what factors are the most

important, but under no circumstances should this decision ever be made by cost alone.

What Are Symptoms?

Simply put, symptoms are indicators of diseases or disorders; because dogs cannot talk, symptoms provide the only signs that your pet is not feeling well. Although understanding the symptoms, or combinations of symptoms, associated with certain ailments may help you narrow down the possibilities, the trained eye of a veterinarian is usually required to determine the exact cause of your Sheltie's illnesses or ailments.

Symptoms to Watch For

There are several symptoms of which every dog owner should be aware. If you notice any one or combination of them, you should call your veterinarian. Be alert for:

- exhaustion
- loss of appetite or thirst
- excessive appetite or thirst
- unusual sneezing or wheezing
- excessive coughing
- runny nose
- discharge from the eyes or ears
- poor coat condition
- foul breath
- blood in the stool
- slight paralysis
- limping, trembling, or shaking
- swelling or lumps on the body
- sudden weight loss
- cloudy or orange-colored urine
- inability to urinate
- uncontrolled urination
- moaning or whimpering

- unusual slobbering or salivation
- vomiting
- diarrhea

The last two, vomiting and diarrhea, are probably the most common of all canine symptoms; however, they do not always indicate the presence of a serious ailment. For example, young dogs sometimes wolf down their food with such speed that their natural defense mechanisms send it right back up again. It is also common to see a dog eat grass and subsequently vomit in a voluntary attempt to purge the digestive tract. While this behavior is completely natural, it may not necessarily be an indicator that a larger problem exists. Persistent vomiting, however, can indicate a very serious ailment and should be reported to your veterinarian immediately. It can be caused by several digestive disorders and diseases and is often accompanied by irregular bowel movements, including diarrhea.

Likewise, the occasional soft stool is usually nothing to worry about. During the warmer summer months, dogs tend to drink more water and, as a result, their stools may become loose or they may even get diarrhea. Short-term acute diarrhea can also be caused by minor stomach upsets. Acute diarrhea starts suddenly and lasts for a few days to a week. Most cases of acute diarrhea can be handled at home by changing your dog's diet. Try using a diet consisting of one-half boiled rice and one-half cooked chicken. Do not restrict your dog's water intake when he has diarrhea, and be sure to keep offering him a clean, fresh supply.

Chronic diarrhea (continuous or frequent watery bowel movements, where your dog is acting sick during the worst bouts), on the other hand, can indicate a serious problem.

Long-standing diarrhea can become a severely debilitating disorder. It can cause your dog's body to lose valuable nutrients, impair immune system functions, and lose his ability to properly detoxify. This can lead to the development of secondary disorders and will become even harder to treat. Whenever you see the signs of chronic diarrhea, it needs to be brought to the immediate attention of your veterinarian.

Immunization: Pros and Cons

Before the discovery of vaccines, several infectious diseases ran rampant through the canine population, leading to a large number of deaths. Thankfully, advances in modern medical science led to the development of vaccines that can protect dogs against the bacteria and viruses that cause most major infectious diseases. While all vaccines are extremely effective, not all are needed by every dog and not all offer permanent protection.

For years the standard practice was to give dogs scheduled booster shots; in some cases, the frequency in which they were given was determined by local law. This "better safe than sorry" practice is presently the topic of heavy debate. Homeopaths have long argued against frequent vaccination, claiming that vaccines are not as benign as first believed and dogs that are vaccinated excessively or needlessly are subject to more diseases and disorders than dogs that are not. In reaction to this, many veterinary schools have begun researching the effects of vaccines in order to determine if the effect they have on the long-term health of the dog outweighs the benefits gained from the presently recommended vaccination protocol.

Another approach being used to determine the need to revaccinate is called "titer" (titre) testing. This test is used to determine the levels of specific disease-fighting antibodies the dog has in his bloodstream. If the titer test reveals sufficient levels of a specific disease fighting antibody, then it is a good indicator that the dog has immunity against the disease and revaccination is not needed. Unfortunately, a low or absent titer does not always indicate that the dog does not have immunity.

A dog's immune system has a "memory" and will not expend energy developing unnecessary antibodies if it has the ability to produce more within a day or two of exposure to an infectious organism. So while titer testing will tell if a dog has a level of antibody to give him a reasonable chance to fight a disease, it can give false negatives that could lead to unnecessary booster vaccinations.

So where does this leave the average dog owner? My recommendation is to treat vaccine administration as a medical procedure and as such, the benefits as well as risks need to be considered when making the decision to use them. Talk to your veterinarian about your concerns. In return, listen to the reasoning he uses in determining the frequency recommended for vaccination (which comes from practical experience). If you believe that your veterinarian has your pet's best interest in mind, then the choice is usually very easy. Keep in mind, however, that sometimes the frequency of vaccination (particularly for rabies) may be required by local law.

Infectious Diseases and Vaccines

In the United States, vaccines are now divided into two classes. "Core" vaccines are those that the American Veterinary Medical Association (AVMA) recommends should be given to every dog, and "non-core" vaccines are limited to certain dogs, depending on their

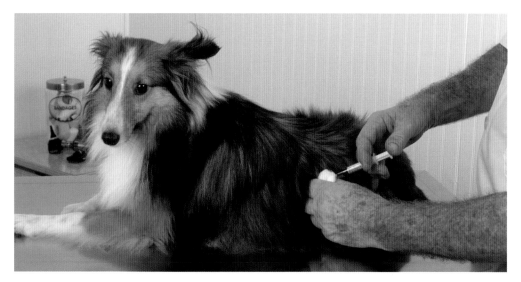

species and environment. The choice to use non-core vaccines depends on a number of variables, including age, breed, the health status of the dog, the potential of exposure, the type of vaccine, and how common the disease is to the geographical area where the dog lives. So, dogs that are not boarded probably do not need all the vaccinations against "kennel cough," and the Lyme disease vaccine should be administered only if you live in an area where it is prevalent. It is important to note that some core and non-core vaccines are given by veterinarians in what are called "combination vaccines." These are single injections that will deliver the vaccines for as many as five different contagious diseases. Determining what "combination" and non-core vaccines as well as the type and frequency of booster immunizations your dog receives is a decision that you will have to make with the advice of your veterinarian.

The four core vaccines will immunize your Sheltie against canine distemper, canine hepatitis, parvovirus, and rabies. Recently, however, a report from the AVMA recommends adding canine adenovirus-2 (presently classified as non-core) to the core vaccines. Non-core vaccines also exist for bordetellosis, parainfluenza, leptospirosis, coronavirus, and Lyme disease. Chances are that your breeder will have your puppy up-to-date on his immunizations when you get him, and your veterinarian can tell you when to schedule additional vaccinations that are necessary.

Worms and Worming

Worms are by far the most common internal parasite found in dogs. There are four major types of worms that live in the digestive tract of the infected animal (roundworms, hookworms, whipworms, and tapeworms) and one major type that attacks the heart muscle (heartworms). The eggs of the digestive tract worms, and sometimes adult worms themselves, can be found in the dog's stool. The eggs are microscopic, so if you suspect your dog has worms, you will have to take a stool sample to the veterinarian so the proper medication can be given.

Digestive Tract Worms

To keep your Sheltie free of digestive tract worms, a stool check should be performed annually by your veterinarian. Early detection and treatment will help prevent malnutrition, diarrhea, and stress-related immune suppression. It will also lessen the risk of transmission of these parasites from pet to pet, as well as from pets to people (especially children).

Symptoms of worm infestation include diarrhea, cramps, irregular appetite, weakness, poor coat condition, bloated belly, blood in the stool, and in severe cases, paralysis. Depending on the identification of the type of worm detected, treatments may be in the form of an oral or injectable dewormer.

Heartworm

While once found only along the southeastern sea coast, heartworm can now be found throughout the United States and is transmitted through bites by mosquitoes. There are presently more than 60 species of mosquito known to transmit this illness. Heartworms spend their adult life attached to the right side of a dog's heart and the large blood vessels that attach the heart to the lungs. They can also be

worms. In addition, if preventives are used when adult heartworms are present, other severe problems can result. It is, therefore, very important to have your dog tested by your veterinarian for the presence of heartworms before any medications are started. If fully grown worms are present, they need to be treated with an adulticide or through surgical procedures.

There are a number of heartworm preventives available, and some will also help control other parasites. It is suggested that preventive medications should be used year-round, even in areas where mosquitoes occur seasonally. If given continuously, the preventive will stop the worms from developing into adults. The choice of medications should be discussed with your veterinarian so you can learn the pros and cons of each.

found in other species of animals but are rarely seen in humans.

Severely infected dogs can host several hundred adult heartworms which can live for five to seven years. This puts a very great strain on an infected dog's heart, that becomes enlarged, has to work harder, ages rapidly, and eventually weakens. Adult worms can obstruct the heart chambers and blood vessels between the heart and lungs. If a worm dies it can block the flow of blood to smaller vessels, thus causing any number of circulation-related problems. Symptoms include coughing, decreased appetite, weight loss, and lethargy. In rare situations where infestations are very severe, the dog may die of sudden heart failure.

The best way to deal with heartworms is to use preventive medications, but it is important to understand that these do not kill the adult

External Parasites

During the course of practically every dog's life, it will experience some form of discomfort that will be caused by external parasites, such as fleas, ticks, or mites. These parasites can be extremely irritating to pets (as well as their owners) and cause serious skin problems. In addition, they can be the carriers of many diseases.

Fleas

The most common of canine parasites, fleas cause more pain and suffering than any other ailment. Fleas flourish when the weather turns warm and humid, so depending on the climate in which you live, fleas may be a seasonal or year-round problem. They differ from other parasites in that their strong hind legs enable them to jump long distances from one dog (or other warm-blooded host) to another. Adult fleas are dark brown and about the size of a sesame seed. They are highly mobile and once they crawl under a dog's thick coat, they can move rapidly over their skin.

It is possible for 10 adult fleas to produce well over 250,000 offspring in a month, so if left untreated, it will only be a matter of time before your Sheltie begins to show obvious signs of discomfort. Symptoms of flea infestation range from mild redness of skin to severe scratching that can lead to open sores and skin infections. Another sign of flea infestation is the presence of small black flea "droppings" (about the size of fine ground black pepper) that the parasite leaves on your pet's coat. The excrement is dried blood meal, so if you put some of the powder on a damp white tissue it will turn a rusty red-brown color as it dissolves. You may also see adult fleas along with the excrement if you use a flea comb on the infested dog.

Fleas feed by biting their host and sucking their blood, so a Sheltie with heavy flea infestations can become anemic. Some dogs are allergic to flea saliva, which results in even more irritation and scratching. Where infestations are very heavy, fleas have been known to bite humans. With modern medicines, prevention of flea infestations is much easier and safer than it was in the past. There are several topical flea adulticides on the market today that are very effective preventives and last up to 30 days per dose. They do not require the flea to ingest blood and can kill the flea before it bites or lays eggs.

Ticks

These dangerous blood-sucking parasites can be found in just about all countries worldwide.

They are of particular concern because some of them carry and transmit disease.

Tick populations and the diseases associated with them vary demographically. The most common tick found in the United States is the "brown dog tick," which is large enough to be seen with the human eye. While not all brown ticks are dangerous, it has been implicated as a carrier of Rocky Mountain spotted fever and babesiosis. These two diseases have similar symptoms including fever, anorexia, depression, lethargy, and a rapid pulse rate. Another disease carrier is the deer tick, which is much smaller and barely perceptible to the human eye. It is this diminutive tick that is responsible for the spread of Lyme disease.

Dogs that frequent grassy and wooded areas populated by wild mammals have the greatest risk exposure to ticks. Both the nymph and adult stages feed on animals. Unfed ticks resemble small crawling bugs, but once they attach themselves and begin to feed on their host, they begin to swell with blood until they look like a dried raisin. As they continue to gorge, they swell like a miniature balloon. Ticks are most often found around a dog's neck, in the ears, in the folds between the legs and body, and between the toes. Tick bites can cause skin irritation, and heavy infestations can cause anemia. If you take your Sheltie to tick-prone areas for fun or exercise, be sure to examine him for ticks immediately upon returning home and remove them from your pet. Prompt removal of ticks is very important because it lessens the chance of disease transmission. Pets at risk for ticks can be treated using preventive tick adulticides. Your veterinarian can recommend the product best suited to your needs.

Lice

Like most external parasites, lice are bloodsuckers whose bite causes irritation. They will spend their entire lives among the hair of their hosts. When they lay their eggs (called nits), they become firmly attached to the victim's hair. If your dog is infested, you can see the egg clusters attached to the hairs. Lice can be very dangerous, so bring your dog to the veterinarian if you spot eggs; he can be readily treated with insecticidal products.

Mites

Mites are very small parasites that do their damage by burrowing into a dog's skin, causing intense itching. Mites are no bigger than a pinhead and require a microscope for proper identification. When they burrow into the skin in large numbers, they can cause a serious skin disease called mange. While mange can occur in healthy dogs, a clean sanitary environment is the best deterrent. This condition is more typically found in dogs that frequent unsanitary places and suffer from improper nutrition.

The symptoms of mite infestations are severe itching and the crusting/scabbing of infected areas. Mange is usually treated using topically applied medications, but in many cases the cleaning and sanitizing of the affected dog's environment is also necessary. Some forms of mange can be transmitted to humans, and people who come into close contact with a carrier dog can develop skin rashes.

Common and Hereditary Ailments

Practically all purebred dogs have a predisposition for many diseases and ailments that are either the result of poor breeding practices somewhere in their genealogy or are due to their anatomical structure, and the Sheltie is no exception. It cannot be stressed enough that breeding practices (heredity), environment, and socialization are all important factors that affect the health of an individual Sheltie. Responsible breeders spend their lifetime building a quality bloodline and certifying the health of their dogs. Some of the quality checks that Shetland Sheepdog breeders attain for their dogs include Orthopedic Foundation for

Animals (OFA) testing for hip dysplasia, Canine Eye Registration Foundation (CERF) certification for hereditary eye ailments, VetGen testing for von Willebrand disease (a form of hemophilia), and multi-drug sensitivity (MDR1) DNA testing. Dogs shown to have any of the genetically linked ailments described here should not be used for breeding for fear of perpetuating the disease.

Eye Disorders

The Sheltie is prone to several genetically linked eye disorders. While veterinarians may be very good at offering advice, you may have to see an eye specialist should your dog be diagnosed with one of these ailments.

Collie Eye Anomaly (CEA)

CEA is an inherited eye disorder caused by the abnormal development of the layer of tissue under the retina of the eye. There is no treatment or cure for CEA. A mild form of the disease is very common in Shetland Sheepdogs. It is easy to recognize with an ophthalmologic exam on puppies between five and eight weeks of age. A more severe form of the disease can result in serious vision loss. In some dogs with CEA, lesions of the eye occur, which can lead to secondary problems such as retinal detachment, hemorrhage, and vision loss, although it rarely results in total blindness. The frequency of this gene mutation in Shetland Sheepdogs in the United States is significantly lower than in European Shelties. The CERF Web site, *http://www.vmdb.org/cerf.html*, has additional information about eye diseases, and dogs that have been tested can have their test results sent in to be included in the database.

Juvenile Cataracts

If left untreated, this ailment can lead to blindness. Cataracts form when the eye lens becomes cloudy or opaque, which causes the dog's vision to become blurred and eventually lost. While old-age cataracts can be found in almost every breed of dog, they are not related to the juvenile form that can plague the young dogs of genetically involved breeds. Juvenile cataracts come in two forms: those that will dissolve and can be treated with cortisone eye drops, and those of the non-dissolving type. Shelties that have the non-dissolving form will need to have an ophthalmologist determine if the retinas are normal before considering surgical removal of the cataract.

Distichiasis

This genetically linked eye disorder is caused when a dog's eyelashes grow incorrectly and come into contact with the cornea. This is very irritating to the victim. Symptoms include squinting, excessive tearing, and inflammation. While electrolysis may be a temporary solution, surgery is usually required to permanently correct the problem.

Progressive Retinal Atrophy (PRA)

This hereditary disease causes specialized dim light receptors located in the retina to slowly deteriorate, which will lead to night blindness; luckily it is not as prevalent in the Sheltie as it is in other breeds. As the disease progresses, it will lead to the deterioration of the bright light receptors, resulting in complete blindness. There are no outward symptoms of this disease, but it is characterized by the Sheltie having trouble seeing in the dark. Because of the slow progression, it is usually not seen until a dog is at least a year old. Unfortunately, there is no treatment for PRA, nor is there any therapy for slowing its progress.

Hereditary Skeletal Disorders

Hip Dysplasia

This inherited development disorder of the hip joints occurs most commonly in large breeds, but it is also seen in the Shetland Sheepdog. The condition is due to a malformation of the hip socket that does not allow the proper fit of the head of the femur. At birth, the hip of the affected dog appears normal and signs of a problem may not appear until the dog is at least five to nine months of age. Hip dysplasia results in the painful inflammation of the hip joint, which leads to permanent physical damage including lameness and loss of the use of the back legs. Over-feeding, over-exercising, and injury can also contribute to a young Sheltie damaging his hips.

Treatment for this ailment is to surgically correct the shape of the hip socket, or to perform a total hip replacement. While these surgeries have a high success rate, they are only performed by a small number of specialists and can be quite costly. If you are planning to breed your dog, be sure to have him certified free of hereditary hip dysplasia by the OFA.

Legg-Calvé-Perthes Disease (LCP)

LCP is a disorder of the hip joint conformation that occurs in both humans and dogs. In dogs, it is most commonly found in smaller breeds between the ages of four and twelve months. The disease results when the blood supply to the "ball" of the joint is interrupted, causing the death of bone cells and a change to the shape of the "ball." Once the blood supply is restored, the "ball" no longer fits correctly in the "socket." The process of bone cells dying and breaking followed by new bone growth and reshaping of the "ball" can lead to stiffness and pain. Symptoms include irritability, chewing of the flank or hip, progressive lameness, stiffness and atrophy of the muscles of the affected limb, and pain when moving the hip. This ailment is most commonly treated through surgical procedures.

Other Hereditary Diseases and Disorders

Von Willebrand Disease

This common inherited disease is a form of hemophilia, a bleeding disorder caused by

defective blood platelet function that does not allow the blood to clot properly. In addition to excessive or continuous bleeding from injuries, symptoms of this disease include nose bleeds, bleeding from the gums, or blood in the urine or stool. All Shelties should be tested for the presence of this disease, as it is extremely important that both you and your veterinarian know if your dog has a blood-clotting defect. If an afflicted dog becomes injured or requires surgery, the veterinarian will need to take special precautions. While there is no cure for this disease, there are several treatment options available, depending on the severity of the disorder. Treatments range from providing blood-clotting medications (such as vitamin K) in oral or intranasal form to extensive plasma transfusions.

Patent Ductus Arteriosus (PDA)

Before birth, the blood flow of the fetus bypasses the lungs, which are not yet needed for breathing. Instead, the blood flows from the right heart chambers to the left through the ductus arteriosus. At birth, pressure changes in the bloodstream should permanently seal the duct, forcing blood to enter the lungs where oxygen can be exchanged. PDA is a failure to close the duct completely, allowing some blood to bypass the lungs. When this happens, a puppy is not getting the proper amount of oxygen absorbed into its bloodstream.

Initially, no symptoms may be apparent, but as the puppy grows and oxygen demands are not met, he will become less active or may be short of breath and collapse. This may be accompanied by a bluish tint to the gums. A veterinarian may be able to hear a turbulent blood flow (sometimes without a stethoscope). Without surgery, dogs suffering from PDA will most certainly live a shorter life than normal. The surgical procedure used has a high success rate and is best performed before the growth of the puppy is affected.

Congenital Deafness

This ailment is caused by a degeneration of the blood supply to the inner ear, three or four weeks after birth. Dogs that suffer from this incurable hereditary disease will usually have coats with a white pigmentation. It can affect one or both ears and has no outward symptoms. Puppies affected with bilateral deafness (both ears) will fail to wake up when loud noises occur. A brainstem auditory-evoked response (BAER) test is used to diagnose deafness in dogs. Bilaterally deaf dogs are difficult to train and may develop behavior problems, as they are easily startled by sudden movements.

Hypothyroidism

Canine hypothyroidism, or the absence of sufficient thyroid hormone to maintain healthy body functions, can be inherited or idiopathic (of no known origin). There are many symptoms of hypothyroidism that can point to the need to be tested to determine the extent of the disease and select the best treatment. These symptoms are often contradictory to one another but include lethargy, skin odor, hair loss, greasy skin, dry skin, weight gain, dull coat, skin infections, constipation, diarrhea, cold intolerance, reproduction problems, and aggression. There are several diseases or conditions that are associated with hypothyroidism, some of which can be quite serious. Treatment of this disease involves drug treatment with close monitoring by a veterinarian.

Canine Multi-drug Resistance Gene Mutation (MDR1)

Shetland Sheepdogs, like most Collie relatives, are known to have a mutation in the multi-drug resistance gene (MDR1), which makes them more sensitive to certain drugs. Dogs with this mutant gene are not capable of pumping certain drugs out of the brain as a normal dog would, which can result in abnormal neurological signs and can even lead to death. Drugs known or suspected to cause problems in dogs with the mutant MDR1 gene include Ivermectin (anti-parasitic agent) and Loperamide (over-the-counter anti-diarrhea agent). Because a Sheltie with a mutant MDR1 gene can be harmed by some drugs that are typically used in the veterinary medicine field, it is important to know if your dog has this mutant gene so that you can inform your veterinarian. Tests can be performed by mailing a cheek swab to a DNA testing laboratory. You can find out more about this ailment and instructions on how to take and send cheek swabs, as well as a complete list of drugs known to (or suspected of having) a negative impact on dogs with the mutant MDR1 gene by going to the following Web site: *www.vetmed.wsu.edu*

Congestive Heart Failure (CHF)

Congestive heart failure is an abnormality in the heart that leads to fluid retention in the lungs and body cavities. There are many causes of heart failure in dogs, including congenital (present at birth) defects of the heart, degeneration of heart valves, disease of the heart muscle, heartworm, and irregular heart beat. Heart failure can develop in dogs of any age and any breed, but many of the older, small-breed dogs develop heart failure from the degeneration of the heart valves. CHF may or may not be genetic.

Heart failure leads to fatigue by reducing the amount of blood that is pumped to the muscles. Most cases of heart failure are associated with accumulation of fluid in the lungs, chest cavity, or abdominal cavity. The symptoms of heart failure include coughing, shortness of breath, difficulty breathing, weight loss, and fatigue. There are several diagnostic tests to confirm the presence of CHF and its underlying cause. Treatment for CHF will vary depending on the cause and may include one or more of the following: treatment with a diuretic, oxygen, and other drugs such as nitroglycerine. If your dog is diagnosed with CHF, you should avoid giving your Sheltie excessive exercise or excitement, high heat/humidity, and foods or treats that are high in salt.

Collie Nose

The term "Collie nose" is used to describe a condition where dogs (not only Collies) with little or no pigment on their face develop scabby lesions around the nose, eyelids, and/or lips. These lesions are caused by a hypersensitivity to sunlight. "Collie nose" can be hereditary and is worse on dogs that live in sunny climates. Left untreated, severe discomfort can result. As the nasal tissues become irritated, they may crack, bleed, and impair breathing. All cases should begin treatment in the early stages. Advanced stages may develop into a form of cancer, which can be deadly. "Collie nose" can be managed several ways. Exposure to sunlight should be kept to a minimum. Sunscreen lotions help but have limited effectiveness due to a dog's licking behavior. In some cases, the treatment of choice is tattooing, where permanent black ink is tattooed into the affected areas. The black ink serves as a shield against sunlight. It is best if young dogs with lightly pigmented noses, as a preventive, are tattooed before any lesions develop.

CHECKLIST

Items to Have in a First Aid Kit
- ✔ Elastic bandages
- ✔ Sterile non-stick dressing
- ✔ Antibiotic cream or ointment
- ✔ Scissors
- ✔ Cotton balls and swabs
- ✔ Antiseptic solutions
- ✔ Saline solution
- ✔ Digital thermometer
- ✔ Sterile ophthalmic ointment
- ✔ Tongue depressors
- ✔ Tourniquet
- ✔ Tweezers
- ✔ Alcohol
- ✔ Adhesive tape
- ✔ Snake bite kit (if you have poisonous snakes where you live)

General Disorders

Constipation

As with humans, constipation in dogs is usually related to dietary issues. A lack of fiber or fresh water can disrupt a Sheltie's digestive system, while ingesting foreign objects, such as bones, rocks, or garbage can also cause intestinal blockages. Constipation can also be caused by a lack of exercise, worm infestations, or medications that a dog may be taking.

The treatment used for constipation is dependant on the cause. If your dog is passing hard, dry stools, you can try adding fresh vegetables or a half teaspoon of bran to each meal to see if the stool softens. Make sure there is always fresh water available to drink, and exercise your dog an hour after each meal. In chronic or severe cases, or when you know the cause is the ingestion of a foreign object, you should bring your dog to the veterinarian immediately.

Hot Spots and Moist Eczema

Also known as summer sores, this ailment can occur anywhere on the body and can spread rapidly. While hot spots can be caused by a variety of factors, the most common is bacterial infections, which can occur any time

a dog's skin becomes irritated and broken. Whenever these infections are provided with a warm moist environment (from baths, wet grass, licking, etc.), they can easily spread. Hot spots do seem to be more prevalent in the summer, most likely because hot weather will promote bacterial growth. It can penetrate very deeply into the skin and cause severe itching, resulting in a dog that excessively scratches and licks in an attempt to gain some relief. This only adds to the spread of the disease.

Hot spots that are bacterial in nature can be treated with oral or topical antibiotics. Because the infection can penetrate deeply into the skin, keeping your Sheltie well-groomed and free of matted hair (or perhaps even shaving the coat) will help keep the problem in check. Providing your dog with a proper diet will help keep his skin and coat in optimum condition and reduce the scratching that can lead to the development of this ailment.

Shock

This condition is caused by lack of blood flow to meet the dog's needs, so any condition that adversely affects the heart or blood volume can induce shock. It can be brought on by hemorrhages, poisoning, and dehydration, but in dogs the most common cause is being hit by a car. The symptoms of shock, which are the result of inadequate blood circulation, are a drop in body temperature, shivering, listlessness, depression, weakness, cold feet and legs, and a weakened pulse.

If your dog is in shock, keep him calm and speak to him in a soft, reassuring voice. If the shock is caused by blood loss from an open wound, you will need to control the bleeding. Let your dog get into a comfortable position

Normal Physiologic Values for a Sheltie

Temperature	Pulse (beats per minute)	Respirations (per minute)
101.5–102.5°F (38.6–39.2°C)	90–120	18–24

that causes the least amount of pain and makes breathing easier. Cover him with a blanket or a coat (but not too tightly) to keep him warm. Because the actions of a dog in shock can be unpredictable, you need to use caution when handling him. As they are small dogs, a sick or injured Sheltie can be carried, but a blanket "stretcher" can also be used to transport him. When possible, splint or support broken bones before moving your dog, and carry him with the injured parts protected. Use a muzzle only when absolutely necessary, as it can impair the dog's breathing, and bring him immediately to a veterinarian.

Broken Bones

Fractures and broken bones are also frequently the result of auto accidents. A dog with a fracture will be in severe pain, so approach him with caution, as he may attempt to bite. If the dog has a compound fracture (where the broken bone has punctured the skin), cover the wound with gauze or a clean cloth to prevent infection, and bring the injured dog to a veterinarian as soon as possible. Any fracture, simple or compound, requires professional attention.

Just as with humans, your veterinarian will use splints, casts, steel plates, and screws to realign the bone and allow it to heal. The treatment used will depend on the severity of the injury, the type of bone that is broken, and the age of the Sheltie. Growing puppies heal faster than geriatric dogs, so your veterinarian may decide to use a cast on a puppy but use pins for the same injury to an older dog.

Bleeding

To control bleeding you should immediately apply direct pressure to the source of the hemorrhage. Any absorbent material or piece of clothing can be used as a compress, including gauze, towels, or shirts. Be sure to muzzle the dog prior to doing so.

Pressure should be applied for no less than five minutes. If bleeding continues after this time, secure the compress using gauze, a belt, panty hose, or a necktie, and immediately seek the help of a veterinarian. If a leg is involved, applying pressure to the upper portion of the limb will help reduce the flow of blood. If a tourniquet is needed, it can be applied just above the wound using a belt, necktie, or panty hose. A pencil, ruler, or thin piece of wood can be used to twist and tighten the tourniquet until the bleeding has minimized. To prevent permanent damage to the leg, you should be able to pass one finger between the tourniquet and the skin without too much effort. You should also release the pressure on the tourniquet for thirty seconds every ten to fifteen minutes.

Poisoning

Humans and dogs live their lives surrounded by poisons and toxins. Dogs, however, cannot read warning labels, which puts them at

TIP

Giving Medication Directly

If you need to use force to get a dog to take his medications, you can use the following advice. Get the pill out, hold it with your thumb and index finger, and call the dog with a happy voice. Place the dog's hind end against a wall so he cannot back away from you. Using your other hand, gently grasp the dog's muzzle from the top with your thumb on one side and your other fingers on the other. Squeeze behind the upper canine teeth and tilt the head back to automatically open his mouth. Use one finger, on the hand holding the pill, to push down between the lower canine teeth, and place the pill as far back into the dog's mouth as possible, making sure to get it over the "hump" of the tongue. Close the dog's mouth and hold it closed, lower the head into a normal position, and gently rub or blow on the dog's nose to help stimulate him to swallow. When you are done, be sure to give the patient plenty of praise and a treat if his diet allows, which will make it easier to do the next time. You can also ask your veterinarian to show you how it is done, because seeing a live demonstration is a great way to learn.

Liquid or oral syringe medications can be given to your dog in much the same way as a pill. Be sure to shake the medicine and have it measured in a syringe or eyedropper before you call the dog. Place the tip of the syringe or eyedropper into the pocket formed between the dog's cheek and back teeth, and slowly administer the medication.

an extreme disadvantage. Most cases of dog poisoning are the result of ingestion; in rare cases, poisoning can occur through inhalation or absorption through the skin. Unfortunately, despite the best intentions of their owners, poisoning is common in dogs because of their curious nature and indiscriminating taste. The amount of damage a poison does is related to the amount the dog ingests (inhales, etc.) and how long it has been in the body before treatment. If treatment is immediate, some poisons will not have any effect, while others, regardless of the speed at which the treatment is administered, can be fatal or result in permanent damage.

The effect of a poison may not always be immediately seen. Some will not cause illness for a few days to a week or more, but most common poisons result in symptoms that can be seen within three to four days of exposure. Because of this time lapse, you should never wait if you see your Sheltie ingesting any potentially harmful substance. If you see your dog ingest anything he should not, read the label for warnings and the proper therapy or antidote you should use. You can call your veterinarian and/or poison control center (whose phone numbers you should always have on your telephone) for the recommended course of treatment. Taking immediate action can sometimes mean the difference between life and death, so there may be some times where you will need to take action yourself; be sure to report all toxic ingestions to your veterinarian as soon as possible.

Some of the most common poisons found in most people's homes include antifreeze, acetaminophen, pesticides, and lead-based paints. Fortunately, most of these have known anti-

dotes, but not all poisons do; therefore, be sure to keep all potentially harmful substances away from your pets, and be sure your Sheltie is not in the area whenever you are using them.

Home Care for the Older Sheltie

As your dog ages, he will experience a gradual decline in his physical and sometimes mental capabilities. Small breeds like the Sheltie usually are considered geriatric between ten and fourteen years old. Like humans, geriatric dogs require special care from their owners to help minimize the effects of the aging process and make their golden years as comfortable as possible.

Make sure that your pet's living and sleeping space is clean, warm, and protected. You should provide soft bedding and limit the changes to the dog's environment, including prolonged changes in temperatures that many geriatric dogs cannot adjust to very well. Older dogs may also have a harder time seeing, so be careful about placing new or potentially dangerous objects in locations where your dog usually moves. You can also consider stomping your feet as you approach your lounging dog to give him a warning of your presence. Should your Sheltie experience stiffening joints or arthritis, you should avoid picking him up unnecessarily, and you may need to consider building ramps that will provide easier access to your home. You can also consult with your veterinarian about using nonsteroidal anti-inflammatory drugs (NSAID), such as ibuprofen, for relief of arthritic pain.

Groom your Sheltie and be sure to brush his teeth regularly; also provide him with the exercise an aging dog still needs to stay in peak health. Grooming helps promote healthy skin and coat and gives the owner the opportunity to perform a home health exam. Check the dog's teeth and mouth for any dental problems or foul odors. Feel the skin for lumps, and look for skin sores or discharge from the eyes and ears. Feel the Sheltie's limbs and abdomen for swelling or signs of pain.

Unless otherwise directed by your veterinarian, routine exercise is very important to the geriatric Sheltie. Walk your dog as often as possible. Even if the dog does not walk well, a short daily walk will help improve his circulation and stimulate the heart muscles, and the

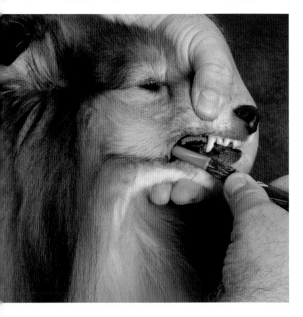

change in environment will provide some mental stimulation.

Be sure that your older dog always has access to fresh, clean water. If your Sheltie is having trouble getting up, it may become necessary for you to bring the water dish to your pet. If your dog does have trouble moving, be extra careful about exposing him to extreme weather, as he may have trouble getting out of the sun or finding a warm corner when the weather gets colder. In these cases you will need to either keep the dog inside, or be sure adequate shelter is nearby. In addition, dogs that have trouble moving or problems with their eyesight should not be left in elevated locations, such as on a table, couch, or stairs, where they could injure themselves trying to get down.

Be careful not to let the older, less active dog become overweight. Feed your aging Sheltie a good quality diet that is appropriate for his aging and mental needs. Avoid giving too many treats, as these can lead to the gaining of unnecessary weight. If your dog always had free access to food, you may need to switch to a once- or twice-a-day program to better monitor food intake. If your dog has teeth problems, it may become necessary to soften his food by adding water to allow hard kibble to soften. Be sure to discuss all instances of unexpected weight gain (or loss) with your veterinarian, who may recommend a specific diet.

As your dog becomes older, you will need to pay even more attention to the indicators of health problems. Symptoms such as irregular breathing, excessive panting, bouts of whining, and weakness in the rear legs are all signs that you need to discuss with your veterinarian. Providing a good home and proper veterinarian care can definitely help your Sheltie live a longer, happier life.

When It Is Time to Say Good-bye

During the course of dog ownership, there is nothing more difficult than seeing your loving and loyal friend become terminally ill. While modern veterinary medicine has many ways to extend the life of our pets, there comes a point where veterinary care will no longer serve a useful purpose. If your dog becomes terminally ill and is experiencing severe and constant pain, aggressive medical attention will not extend his life; instead, it will prolong the dying process. Euthanasia is the act by which a veterinarian painlessly induces death, ending the suffering of a terminally ill animal. When the time comes, you must be ready to consider your pet's feelings as well as your own. This is never an easy choice, but it has been made in the past by millions of pet owners who also loved their pets.

There is no universal process that will help every pet owner through the euthanasia process, and the grief that follows is a different experience for everyone. The most loving and caring of dog owners can become cold and callous, while strong objective owners may completely fall apart. This is a personal experience, and you need to decide what is best for you and your pet.

Most pet owners experience a strong and lasting sense of grief and loss after the passing of their beloved pets. Part of the problem arises because there is no one available who can relate to the personal bond that forms between a dog and his master, and many people feel that talking about it will make them the subject

of ridicule. The bereavement of a loving pet owner can often be self-critical and may even bring up memories of other losses in one's personal life. This can lead to sadness, helplessness, and clinical depression. There is nothing wrong with feeling this way, and as a loving, caring pet owner there is no need to apologize for it. If you feel the need to talk to someone who understands, there is a number of support groups that specialize in pet loss counseling. Never feel ashamed or belittle yourself for the strong feelings you felt for your pet, and know that you are not alone. You can look for these support groups on the Internet, or ask your veterinarian for the telephone number of your local veterinary medical association to be directed to the nearest pet loss specialist.

UNDERSTANDING SHELTIES

The Shetland Sheepdog is an extremely complex creature. To understand his behavior patterns, we must take a close look at the process by which dogs evolved, became domesticated, and were selectively bred to create the wonderful pure breed we know today.

The Nature of Shelties

Earlier we discussed the origins of the Sheltie to see how it acquired its size, shape, and color. To understand the Sheltie's behavior patterns, however, we must examine the process by which dogs evolved and were domesticated. All dogs, regardless of breed, trace their ancestry to a form of wild dog or wolf.

Wild dogs have a specially structured society. Most of their behavior rituals allow each member of the pack to live in harmony with the others. With the passing of countless generations of dogs, some of these rituals became instinctive. Modern domesticated dogs exhibit many of these instinctive behavior patterns, including marking of territory and establishing a ranking order among human companions.

It is believed that dogs were the first domesticated animal; evidence indicates that this process began about 12,000 years ago. Humans probably tamed wolves or wild dogs to assist them in hunting. Hunting practices and social structures of both humans and dogs were probably very similar at this time.

As dogs became domestic, they lost some of their instinctive behavior patterns while others were retained. Which traits were lost and which were retained depends on the specific breed and how it was domesticated. As you know, Shetland Sheepdogs were originally bred as herding dogs, as were most of their domestic ancestors. Thus, Shelties naturally display excellent herding and watchdog skills. While not all of our modern Shelties exhibit all the skills necessary to be an effective herding dog, many of these traits have become part of this breed's instinctive behavioral pattern. An example of this can be seen in the natural movements and temperament of the Sheltie. The physical structure of the Sheltie enables the dog to exhibit strength, speed, grace, and jumping power—all necessary attributes for the successful herding dog. Shelties are also instinctively loyal and affectionate to their owners while showing reserve, but not nervousness, to strangers. All of these traits, with the addition of the Sheltie's alertness, are common to all Shetland Sheepdogs. Yet these features are not seen in all breeds of dogs.

selective breeding. During the last century, breeders have also carefully developed the temperament they deemed desirable in sheepdogs and have tried to eliminate unwanted behavioral problems. For instance, having an aggressive sheepdog would be undesirable. This would frighten the sheep just as much as any predator they might encounter. Therefore, a Sheltie breeder would avoid mating any dogs considered aggressive. Thus, breeders have successfully weeded out many inherent canine behaviors that would be undesirable in a herding dog.

In summary, the nature of the Shetland Sheepdog is a blend of three elements. The first includes all distinctive behavior, such as sexual drive, the marking of territories, and the establishment of a ranking order. The second and third elements result from domestication. They include selectively bred traits and people-oriented traits developed from the shepherd-dog relationship.

Behavior Problems

Because of the care and consistency used by Shetland Sheepdog breeders, relatively few behavior problems are encountered in this breed. In recent years, however, as the popularity of the Sheltie increases, we have also seen an increase in poorly bred dogs. These dogs have been mated by unscrupulous breeders who have obtained the cheapest stud dogs, who care little for the advancement of the breed, and who are doing this only to make a profit. Poor breeding practices usually result in dogs that, besides not meeting the physical requirements of the standard, have behavior problems. These problems include shyness,

Because Shelties and their domestic ancestors were herding dogs, they experienced considerable human contact. Dogs used as sheepdogs must undergo substantial training by a shepherd. This relationship makes the dog into a companion to the shepherd, not just a herding tool. More than other factors, the generations of the shepherd-sheepdog relationship are responsible for the vigilant, obedient, protective, and easy-to-train nature of the Sheltie.

Most of the physical attributes of the Shetland Sheepdog result from generations of

Dog/Human Age Equivalents

Dog's Age	Human's Age	Dog's Age	Human's Age
2 months	14 months	7 years	49 years
3 months	3 years	8 years	56 years
6 months	5 years	9 years	63 years
8 months	9 years	10 years	65 years
12 months	14 years	11 years	71 years
18 months	20 years	12 years	75 years
2 years	24 years	13 years	80 years
3 years	30 years	14 years	84 years
4 years	36 years	15 years	87 years
5 years	40 years	16 years	89 years
6 years	42 years	17 years	95 years

overaggressiveness, or hyperactivity, to name a few.

The major behavior problem associated with the Sheltie is shyness. Although some may not consider shyness in a dog a problem, you must remember that Shelties are herding dogs. Putting a timid dog out in the fields to protect your flock would be ludicrous.

Shyness, however, is not a new problem to the Sheltie breeder. In fact, it dates back to when the dogs were first discovered in the Shetland Islands. It is believed that in the isolation of the islands, Shelties rarely encountered humans beside their owners. These dogs reacted in one of two ways. They were either cautious and watchful of strangers, or they became timid and moved away. So from early in their history, Sheltie breeders have encountered the unwanted trait of excessive timidity.

As a general practice, quality breeders have avoided breeding shy Shelties, and this problem has always been under control. However, because some breeders are ready to compromise for profit, an increase in shy Shetland Sheepdogs has been seen along with the increase of the breed's popularity.

While detecting some shyness in a Sheltie puppy may be possible, many times the extent of this problem cannot be seen until the dog is older. Therefore, be sure to purchase your dog from a reliable and conscientious breeder. Even if you do this, however, your dog may still develop behavior problems. Sometimes controlling this problem is possible through extensive training and counter-conditioning. If, however, you do find that your Sheltie has any problems, be it shyness, overaggression, or any other abnormal behavior, do not mate your dog. While you may still love your dog, for the sake of the breed do not increase the incidence of these problems.

Your Dog's Signals

All dogs use their voices, body language, and facial expressions to convey their emotions. You must pay special attention to these signals to understand your dog's moods.

Dogs do not make noises without a reason. Each sound reflects a mood. A dog will yelp in fright or pain, whine and whimper in loneliness or when seeking attention, groan in contentment or when ailing, and bark in anger or glee. Often you must look for additional signs to determine the purpose of the sounds.

Body language is also a good indicator of a dog's mood. A joyous dog jumps up and down eagerly and may bark. A dog that crouches and lowers his head to the floor is exhibiting fear of being punished, of an intruder, or of another dog. The best indicator of your dog's emotions, however, is his tail. A happy dog wags his tail briskly. The happier he is, the more briskly his tail wags. A frightened dog puts his tail between his legs. An alert or attentive Sheltie raises his tail slightly, while a contented dog has a lowered tail (but not between his legs).

Finally, watch your Sheltie's ears and muzzle, for they are a primary means of facial expression. A contented Sheltie has a closed mouth and normal-set ears. An alert, aroused, or attentive dog picks up his ears. Often your dog will cock his head inquisitively to one side or the other. Be wary of any dog whose ears are back, upper lips are raised, mouth is open, and growling. Although you will rarely see a Sheltie in this position, remember that these are all warning signals of fear and/or anger, and they may precede an attack.

Sense Organs

Dogs in general rely heavily on the senses of smell, hearing, taste, and touch and less on the sense of sight. Like other features, sense organs in a particular breed have been developed through selective breeding and domestication.

The sense of smell is very important to a Sheltie. This sense enables him to find food, locate a mate, and decipher territories.

The area of the olfactory system concerned with smell is more than 40 times larger in a Sheltie than in humans. In addition, Shelties can remember thousands of odors and can associate them with the appropriate people, animals, and places.

Shelties also possess a highly developed sense of hearing, superior to that of humans. They hear a wider range of sounds, especially high-pitched frequencies, such as those emitted from a Galton whistle (silent dog whistle). Shelties hear sounds from a much greater distance than do humans. Their acute hearing is also important to their usefulness as herding dogs. Many shepherds train their dogs to perform commands at the sound of various whistle codes. They do this because high-pitched whistle sounds can travel farther and even during stormy weather can be heard more clearly by the sheepdog.

The Sheltie's peripheral vision is much greater than that of humans. However, their eyes do not focus as sharply as do those of humans. As a result, their eyes are much more sensitive to motion. However, they must rely more on smell and sound to interpret what they see.

Because Shelties possess a long, thick, two-layered, weather-resistant coat, their bodies may appear to lack some sensitivity. However, the body parts not covered by this thick coat, such as the muzzle and nose, do seem to have a high degree of feeling.

Like other dogs, Shelties possess other senses that we still do not understand completely. For example, they have an innate sense of direction. We have all heard reports of dogs traveling hundreds of miles to return home.

As Your Puppy Matures

Additional insight into your Sheltie can be gained when you examine the dog's aging process. As your dog goes through the various stages of his life, he will undergo both physical and emotional changes. The first major change will occur when the young puppy is removed from his littermates and placed into what is expected to become his permanent home.

From the time a puppy is born until he is in his seventh week, he leads a quiet and secure life in the presence of his mother, brothers, and sisters. At the point when the puppy is relocated in his new home, he is becoming much more aware of the world around him. A puppy at this age is very curious, mischievous, and also very impressionable. Training serves as a method of satisfying his curiosity and enables the puppy to learn the rules of his new home. Training will also help the puppy differentiate between playtime and serious time.

Around this time in a puppy's life, he is also becoming more aware of his own physical attributes. Even before you bring your puppy home, he will have already begun to have mock fights with his littermates. This serves to build up strength and to improve motor skills.

When you bring your puppy home, you should immediately start training your puppy. This will help him adapt to his new household. If you wait too long, you will allow this impressionable little creature to pick up bad habits, some of which you may never uproot.

By the time your puppy is 12 or 13 weeks old he reaches what I refer to as the questioning stage. The questioning stage for a puppy is similar to that point when a human child asks "Why is the sky blue?" shortly followed by "Why this?" and "Why that?" In your puppy's case, he has become completely aware of himself and his environment. His favorite pastime will be to share his discoveries with you. He will begin to investigate everything, primarily with his teeth. At this time, he begins to lose his baby teeth and get his permanent ones. Remember that your puppy is still very impressionable, so treat him with care, and continue to reinforce the basic rules of your house.

At seven to ten months old, your puppy will have almost reached his full adult size. This is also when the dog reaches sexual maturity, the equivalent of human adolescence. His once

innocent curiosity will have changed into a bold and assertive interest. This is also a time when, as a teenager might do, your dog begins to test the system. At this point, your Sheltie should be much more comfortable with your lifestyle and will feel he should be included in all your activities. Your Sheltie should know exactly what you expect of him and how he should behave. However, he will naturally try to challenge you to improve his rank. This is, after all, a part of his instinctive canine behavior. When this happens, do not lose your temper. Just teach your Sheltie calmly and firmly that you are the authority. In doing this, you can lead your dog through his final stage of development.

Once your Sheltie reaches maturity, he probably will not undergo any behavioral changes (with the exception of mating urges) until he reaches a ripe old age. Your consistency and evenness of temper in training your dog should now pay off with many years of companionship with a loving, devoted, and trustworthy Shetland Sheepdog.

Changes that occur in the geriatric years depend more on the individual dog and on his medical background. With many old dogs, changes in their daily routines or behavior are often due to a medical problem brought on by old age. As your dog ages, his digestive and immune systems slowly begin to deteriorate.

====== T I P ======

When to Be Wary

Be wary of any dog that has his ears back, upper lips raised, mouth open, and the hair on the back of his neck raised. These are all warning signs of fear and/or anger, that may precede an attack.

The long-term results can include circulatory, musculoskeletal, and nervous system problems. Thus, your older dog might become lethargic or moody, lose his orientation, or experience hearing loss. He may even forget learned responses. This may all sound dreadful, but it is simply a part of the aging process. You cannot do much except try to understand.

Outside Encounters

As part of his heritage as a sheepdog, a Sheltie must learn not to fear people. It is normal for a Sheltie to be wary of strangers, but a sheepdog should never display fear. You can help your dog overcome this problem by introducing him to the outside world and the ways of other humans while he is still very young. In addition to removing the feelings of fear, this will also help your dog learn to behave properly when you have visitors.

On occasion, take your dog with you when you shop. Exposure to strange places and people (as long as you accompany him) will help increase the puppy's confidence in himself and in you. Also take the dog on short car trips. Gradually lengthen the trips until the puppy is used to traveling. A familiarity with travel will make future vacations with your dog much more pleasant.

When you travel by car, keep your dog in a small crate to prevent him from getting in your way and to protect him from injury from sudden stops. You should never leave your dog in the car in hot weather. Even with the windows open, heat builds up very rapidly and can result in heatstroke and death.

In order to truly familiarize your puppy with the ways of the world, walk him (on a leash) in areas where you are likely to encounter other humans and other dogs as well. Allow your puppy to have contact with other humans, as long as that person does not mind. As the teacher, you must show no hesitation toward an approaching stranger. Sometimes your dog can sense this hesitation and will interpret it as a reason to shy away.

When any two dogs encounter each other, they will inevitably try to establish a ranking order. In most cases, this is determined through a mock fight (usually looking like playful wrestling) whereby one dog ends up lying on its back in a subordinate position. However, if neither dog is willing to back down, a real fight might ensue, so be prepared for this possibility. If either dog displays a threatening posture or growls in anger, remove your dog immediately.

If you should encounter another dog, restrain your puppy until the strange dog approaches him. If the two dogs wag their tails and then sniff each other's nose and tail, you can assume that they like each other. Encourage your Sheltie to play with the other dog. Playing will make your Sheltie feel more comfortable in strange surroundings.

BASIC AND ADVANCED TRAINING

Like most herding dogs, the Shetland Sheepdog is relatively easy to train. Several hundred years of close shepherd-sheepdog relationships have imprinted on this breed a strong desire and willingness to learn and perform.

Like almost all of the herding dogs, Shetland Sheepdogs are relatively easy to train. This is because the hundreds of years of shepherd-dog relationships have imprinted the Sheltie with an innate willingness to learn. For this reason, you can begin to train a Sheltie at a much earlier age than many other breeds. In addition, if you conduct your training program properly, you will be able to keep your Sheltie puppy's attention for a longer period of time, thus leading to quicker learning.

Bear in mind that this chapter does not describe all the skills a Sheltie can learn. In fact, I believe that if you have the time, patience, and energy, you can teach your Sheltie an endless number of skills. You must, however, be able to communicate your ideas to your eager student.

Why Dogs Learn

Dogs are pack animals. Because they hunt and live as a group, dogs must learn to coexist in order to survive. This coexistence depends on ranking order. Each dog has a place in the ranking order, usually based on strength and experience. In the pack, all dogs submit to a dog of higher authority. Similarly, a domesticated dog submits only to a higher ranking authority.

During your training sessions you will need to establish your role as the "alpha" pack leader and let your pupil know that he is a subordinate. Once his social rank is established, you will find that your Sheltie will pay greater attention to your commands and show a great eagerness to perform them properly.

Through training, a puppy learns that you are the authority and that the other members of your family rank higher than he does. In addition to establishing ranking order, training teaches your puppy the rules of your house. Teaching a puppy actions and behaviors that are not instinctive takes patience, understanding, and love. You must be consistent and authoritative yet must never lose your temper. Try to understand that human ways are unfamiliar to your Sheltie puppy but that he is eager to learn. Your puppy depends on you to find the proper way to teach him. Once you find the right method, your puppy will respond eagerly and joyfully.

Basic Training Rules

The ten rules listed here will help to set up a good training program for your Sheltie puppy. Each time you begin a training session, make sure you adhere to these rules. This will assure that you give your puppy the best chance to learn his lessons as thoroughly and rapidly as possible.

1. Begin working with your puppy the day you bring him home. Hold two or three sessions a day, and hold them for as long as the puppy shows interest. In 10 or 15 minutes, you can provide sufficient teaching without boring the dog. Your puppy may need two weeks or longer to begin understanding some of your commands, so do not neglect your training.

2. Be consistent. All of the members of your household must decide what is permitted behavior and what is not. For instance, one person should not be teaching the dog to beg for food while the others are teaching the dog not to hang around the dinner table. Once your dog has learned a lesson, never allow him to do the contrary without a verbal reprimand.

3. Be authoritative. Your dog will understand tones better than words. You must deliver all visual and verbal commands clearly and unmistakably. Verbal reprimands must be sharp and firm, while praise must be calm and friendly. While the dog must learn that you are in charge, never demonstrate your authority by using physical force. In addition to being totally unnecessary, forcing your dog to perform or hitting him will teach your dog only to dislike his training sessions.

4. Hold each training session in an atmosphere conducive to learning. Be sure there are as few distractions as possible, and never attempt to teach your puppy anything when you are in a bad mood. Your negative attitude will only confuse the puppy and make learning harder.

5. Do not attempt to teach your puppy more than one new lesson in a single session, and never move to a new concept until the dog has mastered the previous one. Puppies, like people, learn at their own pace and should never be rushed. Once a lesson has been mastered, it can be included as a warm-up exercise in your dog's training regimen.

6. Praise your dog generously for his successes. Verbal praise, petting, or scratching behind the ears will make your Sheltie an eager student.

7. Punish disobedience immediately. Since a puppy has a very short memory, you must never put off a reprimand. If, for example, your puppy chews a slipper, do not punish him unless you catch him in the act; otherwise he will not understand why you are displeased. An adult dog that knows better, however, can be disciplined for the same offense after showing him the slipper.

8. Limit punishments to verbal reprimands. In extreme cases, you can confine your dog to his crate after giving him a verbal reprimand.

9. Even when your dog is older, keep your training sessions short. End them early if the dog begins to lose interest.

10. Never hold a training session when your dog is tired. A tired or exhausted dog will not be attentive. Make it a practice to hold your training sessions before you feed your Sheltie, as he will be less likely to be sleepy or sluggish.

Using Treats During Training

For many years I avoided using treats when training my dogs for fear of creating a pet that expected a food reward for doing what he was told to do. I guess that I am proof that you can "teach an old dog new tricks." In working with many professional trainers I have learned that while some dogs need only our approval or a pat on the head as a reward for good behavior, others need a little more incentive to respond consistently to our commands. For the dog that proves more difficult to train, I have found that using treats during the early training phase is a good way to reinforce the desired behavior, provided they are used correctly.

To prevent your Sheltie from becoming dependent on treats for behavior that is expected of him, I recommend limiting treat-giving to the early phase of training, and only if the dog is having trouble grasping the command. For instance, if you are having trouble getting your puppy to lie down, try placing the treat by your dog's nose and slowly lower it to the floor while you give the "*Down*" command verbally. When he lies down, reward him with the treat. Repeat until you are confident he understands what behavior is expected when you issue the "*Down*" command. As you advance into the later training phases, replace the treat with verbal praise and petting. The goal is to have him respond to your command

in order to receive praise and avoid a verbal reprimand. You can occasionally give a treat during this phase, but do not let him see it until he responds correctly to the verbal command. Many professionals recommend that the only time you should ever consider using a treat throughout training is for the "*Come*" command. This is the most difficult command to teach and you may need every tool in your

toolbox to get your dog to respond consistently. You have to make him want to come to you, and a treat—together with praise—is often the reason he will choose you over any other potentially harmful temptations that your Sheltie may encounter.

Puppy Training

As previously mentioned, training begins the day you bring your puppy home. The longer you wait, the more difficult it will be for your puppy to learn. First teach your Sheltie his name. If you always address your puppy by name, you will be amazed at how fast he will learn this lesson. Make sure your Sheltie does

not hear nicknames. This will confuse him, and he will not respond when called.

Another important lesson is the meaning of "*No.*" Your puppy will probably have to begin learning this lesson his first day at home. As your puppy first explores your home, he will probably do something wrong. When he does, tell him "*No*" in a sharp, firm tone that shows you are serious. If your puppy refuses to listen, pick him up and place him into his crate. Never hit your puppy, either with your hand or with a rolled newspaper, for this will make your puppy hand-shy. Using a crate will simplify training. In addition, as you will see later, it will also speed the process of housetraining.

Being Alone

A puppy must learn early that he will be left alone on occasion. You must teach him to behave properly while you are away, for a poorly trained puppy can cause great damage.

To accustom your puppy to being alone, leave him in a familiar room. Then go into another room where the puppy can neither see nor hear you. Stay there for a short while and then return. If your puppy has done anything wrong, reprimand him. Gradually increase the time you leave the dog in the room alone.

If you must leave before you can trust your puppy alone, lock him in his crate with food, water, and toys until you return. If you do not have a crate, lock him in a familiar room. Remove all tempting objects, including shoes, papers, and clothing. Make sure you leave the puppy his bed and an ample supply of food, water, and toys.

Do not leave a very young puppy alone in your yard, where too many uncontrollable factors exist. Children may tease the puppy, and other animals may be able to bother or hurt him.

No Begging Allowed

To some people, seeing a dog beg looks like a cute and innocent act. Unfortunately, begging is a bad habit for a puppy to develop, and it should never be condoned. Begging may start very innocently. You will be sitting down at the table, about to begin eating a thick steak, when you notice something out of the corner of your eye. It is your faithful puppy, waiting patiently nearby, staring at you with pleading eyes. Now is when most people make their big mistake. They will call the dog over and reward him with a table scrap. You would be amazed at how much a simple act could turn into a nasty habit. While having your Sheltie as a constant table companion may not bother you, it may bother others who are guests in your house.

If your Sheltie attempts to beg for scraps, you must scold him with a sharp *"No!"* and point away from the table and toward the puppy's crate or sleeping box. Within a few weeks, your puppy will learn to avoid the table during mealtimes.

Walking on a Leash

You should start to teach your puppy how to walk on a leash from the first day you bring him home. Before you even bring the puppy into your home, you will be taking him for a walk around your yard to let him relieve himself. Place a collar on the puppy, making sure it is neither too tight nor too loose. Attach a leash, and take your puppy for his first walk. Hold the leash on your left side, and use gentle persuasion to keep your puppy close to your leg. Do not allow the puppy to get under your feet and do not let him run ahead of you. Remain patient. A Sheltie puppy's legs are very short, and the dog is not capable of tremendous speed. If your puppy falls behind, do not attempt to drag him forward. Use friendly words, patience, and a little bit of gentle force to keep your puppy in his proper walking position.

Unnecessary Barking

Barking is one of the most common problems of canine behavior. It is, of course, a natural response for almost all dogs. Even though barking may have numerous causes, including behavioral problems, this section deals with some corrective approaches you can take to help break bad learned behaviors.

Barking is often the sign of alarm. Because of this, you may not want to curb any of your Sheltie's watchdog tendencies. Therefore, discovering whether any of your dog's bad barking habits are an inherited problem or a learned behavior is important. (Inherited problems are discussed in the Understanding Shelties chapter, page 67.)

A learned behavior, for example, is one where the dog barks upon hearing the command *"Speak."* If a dog has been trained by getting food after he speaks, then a dog may speak on his own in order to get a reward. This habit can be broken by *never* giving a dog a reward after he is told to speak. This method is called extinction and relies on the trainer repeating the command over and over but never, ever giving the dog a reward (outside of verbal praise and petting).

This type of training is normally very effective in stopping any bad learned behaviors (such as barking to get into or out of the house, barking to receive food or attention, and so forth). However, be warned. Breaking such bad habits may take a lot of time and patience.

Simple Commands

The first commands to teach your dog are *sit, stay, come,* and *heel.* Teach these commands using these words, and not phrases like *"Come over here, Sparky."* Your dog does not understand complete sentences but rather relies on the command word, your tone, and your gesture. Do not try to teach your Sheltie these commands for long periods of time. Training for short periods two or three times a day is better. Train before you feed the dog, because afterward he may be sluggish. Also, make sure to walk the dog before training. To avoid distractions, train your puppy in a confined area with an audience.

Sit: Take your puppy into an isolated room and fit him with a collar and leash. Hold the leash with your right hand, and place your left hand onto the puppy's hindquarters. Then give the command *"Sit!"* or *"Sit, Sparky!"* in a firm voice, at the same time pressing gently and steadily on his hindquarters. Gently pull the leash upward to keep your puppy from lying down on the floor. Hold the dog in this position for a while. Do not allow him to jump back up.

Do not expect your Sheltie to master this command after the first training session. Repeat the procedure for the entire session or until the puppy begins to lose interest. Remember to praise his efforts each time he sits properly. If you repeat the procedure every day, your Sheltie will soon learn this command.

Once your puppy has performed the sit at least a couple of times in succession, remove the leash and give the command. If your dog has been properly trained, he will perform cor-rectly. If not, remain patient and try again with the leash on.

If you want to use your Sheltie for herding, teach him to respond to a hand signal and to whistles as well. In the field, your dog may be at a distance where he can see you but not hear you. This way your dog can understand your command even if noise prevents him from hearing you. In addition, the sharp sounds of whistles are easier than verbal commands for your dog to hear and interpret from a distance. Once your puppy has mastered the command, hold up either your hand or a single finger in a distinct gesture, and say *"Sit,"* making sure the dog can see the signal. Always use the word (or sound) and the gesture together so your dog connects the two.

Stay: This a more difficult command to teach your puppy, for he will always want to be at your side. The *stay* command orders your dog to remain still wherever he is. This command may someday save your dog's life.

In teaching your dog to stay, first fit him with a leash and collar. Then run through the *sit* procedure and follow it with the command *"Stay."* As you say this new command, raise your hand, palm toward the dog, like a police officer stopping traffic. Each time your dog attempts to stand up, reproach him with a sharp *"No!"*

Take up all the slack in the leash to hold your dog in place. Repeat the procedure until the dog appears to understand. Then remove the leash and repeat the command several times. Praise the dog each time he obeys. If he disobeys, reprimand him.

Continue this command until your Sheltie has repeated the act with regular success. Then, slowly back away from the dog, making sure

to maintain eye contact. While you are moving backward, keep repeating the word *"Stay."* The verbal command should be accompanied by the proper hand gesture. If your Sheltie attempts to follow, give him a loud, sharp *"Stay!"* If the dog continues to follow you, reprimand him. Of course, a dog that stays when told deserves great praise. The *stay* command is sometimes difficult for a devoted puppy to obey because he will always have the urge to be by your side.

Come: If you call out your puppy's name, he will probably race across the room to greet you. The trick to the *come* command, however, is to have your Sheltie obediently come to you when something of greater interest is attracting his attention. *Come* is another command that can protect your dog from dangerous situations.

You should teach the command *come* to your puppy right after *sit* and *stay*. Start by running through the *sit* and *stay* procedures. Once he has stayed at a good distance, call the dog by name and follow with the command, *"Sparky, come!"* Accompany your words with a lively sound or gesture like clapping your hands or slapping your thighs. This will help to excite your dog into motion.

Your Sheltie will quickly associate the word *come* with your movements. Praise him for responding correctly. If he does not respond to the command, put him on a long rope, and let him wander off. Then slowly reel in the rope while repeating the word *"Come!"* Shower your dog with praise when he reaches you. Repeat this exercise several times; then try it without the rope again. Luckily, most Shelties never require this rope exercise.

Obedience Training

The obedience exercises are important for several reasons. Each of the exercises is a requirement for your dog to perform should you enter him into an Obedience competition. However, some of the lessons, such as heeling or relinquishing an object, are important for all dogs to learn. They will allow you to handle your dog properly in awkward situations and will help to reinforce your dog's understanding of the master/subordinate relationship.

Obedience Schools

Contrary to popular belief, obedience schools are not schools for wayward dogs. Instead, they are where, in the proper atmosphere, your dog can learn all he must know to compete in shows. Even if you do not plan to enter your Sheltie into an Obedience trial, these schools offer an enjoyable, interesting, and easy alter-

native to training your dog alone. These schools are run by experienced dog handlers who can supply you with expert advice and invaluable training tips.

An older child in the family should be the one to take your Sheltie to obedience classes. This allows the child and dog to spend more time together. It also teaches your child how to care for a dog responsibly. Working with a dog at obedience school will teach your child both greater self-respect and respect for the dog.

Check with your Shetland Sheepdog Club and the AKC for a reputable obedience school in your area. Before enrolling your dog, make sure the class suits your purpose. Most schools offer special classes for owners interested in showing their dogs, and others for amateurs. Remember that obedience schools can be costly, depending on the problems your dog presents.

Heeling

When your Sheltie heels properly, he will walk on your left side with his head about the same distance forward as your knees. When you begin teaching your dog this lesson, you will require the leash. Eventually, your Sheltie must learn to heel without the restraint of the leash.

To start, run through all the other commands your dog has mastered. This will give your dog extra confidence before you start this difficult lesson. Hold the end of the leash in your right hand, and grab about halfway toward the collar with your left hand. Begin a brisk walk (by your dog's standard) giving the sharp command *"Heel"* or *"Heel, Sparky!"* Use your left hand to control and guide. With this new command, your dog may act rather unpredictably at first, but be patient.

If your dog lags behind, pull steadily on the leash to bring it even with your leg. Do not drag the dog forward or force him to obey your commands, for this will destroy the well-established learning atmosphere. If your dog runs forward, pull him back to your side and give the *heel* command again. If you have difficulty getting your dog to perform correctly, run through the old *sit* and *stay* exercises. Whenever your dog responds correctly, praise him. When he reacts improperly, reprimand him immediately. When he has performed the *sit* and *stay* correctly, begin the *heel* exercises again.

The *heel* lesson is very difficult for a dog to learn. Take your time, be patient, and do not try to teach your dog too quickly. Once your Sheltie has mastered the *heel* on a leash, take him through a turning exercise. If he has trouble heeling while you turn, then take a shorter grip on the leash, and bring the dog closer to your side. Then repeat the command *heel* in a sharp tone, and gently persuade him to follow you by lightly pulling on the leash. As your Sheltie improves in this lesson, take him through a series of straight line, right turn, and left turn exercises. Once he has mastered turning, you can begin training with a slack leash.

Go through the heeling exercises with the leash exerting no pressure on your dog's collar. At the dog's first mistake, grasp the leash firmly and lead the dog steadily in the proper direction. When your dog performs correctly, remember to praise him.

When your dog has learned to walk correctly with a slack leash, remove the leash completely. If he has performed properly with a loose leash, you should be able to achieve the same results without the leash. Do not allow your Sheltie to regress into any bad habits. If the dog does not perform properly, then verbally reprimand him. If you continue to have trouble, you will have to put the leash back on. Repeat the *heel* lesson, then try again without the leash. If you repeat the lessons carefully, and have the exact same routine with and without the leash, your dog should eventually learn to heel properly. Always remember to praise a job well done. This will help to reinforce your Sheltie's good behavior.

Relinquishing an Object

Every good dog must learn to give up any object obediently, if his master so desires. Shelties are no exception. This lesson is important in teaching your dog his subordinate role.

Begin by giving your Sheltie a suitably sized piece of nonsplintering wood to hold in its teeth. Then command your dog to sit, praising him when he obeys. While using both hands, slowly pull the dog's jaws apart while saying *"Let go"* in a strict and firm tone. If your dog begins to growl, give him a sharp *"No!"* Do not be afraid if your Sheltie growls. This is a dog's way of trying to establish his dominance and a natural reaction to anyone who attempts to take away his prey. You must, however, make your Sheltie clearly understand that you are the boss, and take the object away. Once your dog accepts you as a dominant force, he will give up the stick without any objection.

Lying Down

Have your dog assume a sitting position (which should be easy by now). Then slowly pull his front legs forward while saying *"Down!"* If your dog attempts to stand up, give him a sharp *"No!"* If pulling on his front legs does not work, then slowly pull them forward and push down on the dog's shoulders at the same time.

While you do this give the command *"Down!"* Because you will have both hands occupied, you can carefully step on the leash to prevent the dog from returning to his feet. Keep the dog in the lying position for about one minute. Gradually increase this time period as your dog progresses. When your dog has mastered this lesson, begin to move away. As you do this, you must maintain constant eye contact with your pupil. Whenever the dog attempts to stand up, repeat the command *"Down!"* in a firm, sharp tone. Repeat the lesson until you are satisfied with your Sheltie's performance.

Retrieving

Retrieving is an unusual act for any Shetland Sheepdog to perform. However, you may be surprised at the number of Shelties who perform this feat as if it were instinctive. On the other hand, I have met several other Shelties that would attempt to herd a ball back to their owners by encircling it and barking rather than picking it up in their mouths and returning it obediently.

With proper training, any young Sheltie can learn the art of retrieving. Throw a suitably sized nonedible ball or stick, with your dog standing next to you, and call out *"Fetch."* Provided that you did not throw the object clear out of the dog's sight, he will most likely run after the object.

If the dog picks up the object in his mouth and returns to you, command the dog to sit, put out your hand, palm up, under his lower jaw, and say, *"Let go!"* You should be able to remove the object from the dog's mouth without any resistance. If your dog drops the object, place it back into his mouth, and then remove it, saying *"Let go!"*

If your Sheltie shows no desire to return with the object, repeat the exercise using a 30-foot (9-m) rope. Tie the dog to the cord, throw the object, and call out *"Fetch!"* again. Once he has picked up the object, draw the dog toward you. Then take the object from the dog.

If your dog hesitates in picking up the object, place the object into his mouth and follow the commands for relinquishing an object. Keep repeating this lesson until the dog understands that he must take this object into his mouth. Then throw the object only a short distance to see if the dog will pick it up. With patience and persistence, you can teach your Sheltie to perform this command as well as if he were a Retriever bringing a hunter his prey.

Jumping Over Hurdles

This may not be as difficult a lesson as you may think (provided the hurdles are Sheltie sized). Herding dogs must know how to jump over obstacles, if need be, to prevent a flock from scattering. You may find that your dog will learn this lesson with relative ease. First, command your dog to sit on one side of a small pile of boards while you stand on the opposite side. Command the dog by saying, *"Jump!"* If he walks around the obstacle, say *"No!"* then bring him back and start over. Praise your dog for a successful performance.

As your dog learns to jump on command, begin a jump and retrieve exercise. Place the object to be retrieved on the other side of the hurdle. Command your dog to sit next to you. Then command him to retrieve the object by saying, *"Jump! Fetch!"* in a clear, firm voice. The dog should leap over the obstacle, pick up the object, and jump back with it. Tell the dog to sit again. Then take the object out of its mouth by

saying, *"Let go!"* Praise your dog warmly for his accomplishments.

Problems in Training

No two Shetland Sheepdogs are precisely alike. Each has his own idiosyncrasies. Individual learning abilities can vary greatly. The key in training is to establish the proper rapport with your dog. As I have stated earlier, the training exercises described in this book are merely outlines for teaching commands. You have the responsibility, as your dog's trainer, to establish an effective system of communication. This will make it easier for your Sheltie to understand your commands and perform them well.

If you reach a point when your Sheltie has trouble learning a lesson, remain patient and understanding. Never try to force your Sheltie to learn. Anger and beating have never helped a dog learn anything! They only serve to create an atmosphere not conducive to learning. Eventually, this will cause your Sheltie to lose trust in you.

When you and your pupil hit a roadblock, start by examining your teaching methods. Review the ten basic rules of training (pages 76–77), and correct any mistakes that you may have been making. In most cases, you will find that your teaching method was causing the problem.

If, after thoroughly reviewing your methods, you feel that this is not the problem, carefully examine your dog and his environment. Your Sheltie could possibly be distracted by an outside factor. If so, then you must remove the distraction. Could your dog be ill? If illness is suspected, make an appointment to see your veterinarian.

Should you continue to run into training difficulties, I strongly recommend that you contact a reputable obedience school. In many instances, the human ego will not allow us to believe that we could be doing anything wrong. Professional dog handlers who run these training facilities can usually spot problems rather easily.

By starting early and working hard, you will most assuredly be able to train your Sheltie to whatever stage you desire. Only as you grow older with your Sheltie will you begin to understand the importance of proper training and begin to reap its rewards. Through diligence and establishment of a harmonious training atmosphere, you and your faithful four-legged companion will enjoy many wonderful years of camaraderie.

The Shetland Sheepdog in Competition

Many Sheltie owners are attracted to participating in dog shows because it combines the excitement of competition with a chance to spend more quality time with their dogs. In the United States the AKC sponsors many events that attract millions of participants. These events include conformation shows, obedience trials, field trials, hunting tests, agility trials, Canine Good Citizen tests, lure coursing, herd-ing trials, and tracking tests. While Shelties are technically able to compete in many of these events, it's most common to find them competing in conformation shows, Good Citizen tests, herding trials, and agility trials.

It is important to learn about each event and decide which ones you would like to participate in before you decide to have your pet spayed/ neutered. Some events, such as conformation shows, prohibit spayed/neutered dogs from participating, while others have special application rules for spayed/neutered pets. You can learn more about all of the rules by visiting the AKC Web site.

Should you decide to try the show ring, keep in mind that no individual dog can please everyone. While it would be great if your Sheltie delighted each judge he met, you should not count on this happening, for dogs of that caliber are extremely rare. It is much more important that your dog pleases you. Never blame your dog for failure in the ring, for if it were up to your Sheltie, he would win every award possible to please you. Go to the shows, have a good time, and learn all you can. Afterward, bring your beloved companion back home and show him that you still believe that he is the best dog in the world.

Conformation Events

Conformation events are shows in which the quality of the breeding stock is evaluated (thus the reason a spayed/neutered dog cannot compete). In these shows, a Sheltie would be judged on his appearance, physique, bearing, temperament, and how well the dog conforms to the breed standard.

There are three types of conformation dog shows: all-breed shows, specialty shows for a specific breed, and group shows that are limited to dogs belonging to one of the seven AKC groups (Working, Herding, Sporting, Non-sporting, Hounds, Terrier, and Toy). Naturally, Shelties would compete in the Herding group. The AKC also offers children from 9 to 18 years of age the opportunity to compete in junior showmanship events. Here, the juniors are judged on how well they present their dogs.

If you are interested and want to know more about conformation shows, you can start by joining a local kennel club that will have information on training classes for the show ring, or by contacting the AKC for more information. You should also attend a show as a visitor. If the grooming area is open to the public, talk to professional groomers to get some tips. If you are considering the purchase of a Sheltie, you will have the benefit of many expert breeders and exhibitors to talk to. You can also find pet product vendors and club booths that often offer helpful information. Once you know what to expect, you can better enjoy the experience of competitive dog shows.

Canine Good Citizen Test

The Canine Good Citizen test is an evaluation of the dog's ability and willingness to behave and act properly in public. This test ultimately reflects the handler's own ability as a trainer. In addition, this is the only AKC-sponsored activity that allows mixed-breed dogs to participate. Ten different tests are administered on a pass-fail basis. If you and your Sheltie pass all ten of the following tests, you can apply for a Canine Good Citizen certificate and collar tag.

• **Accepting a friendly stranger:** Your Sheltie must show no signs of aggression, shyness, or jealousy when approached by the evaluator.

He must not break his position or jump on the evaluator either.

• **Sitting politely for petting:** Your dog must sit still when the evaluator approaches and then pets him.

• **Appearance and grooming:** Your dog should calmly allow both grooming and hands-on examination by the evaluator. He is allowed to move during the test but should not struggle.

• **Out for a walk:** Your pet should maneuver on a loose leash without pulling, struggling, or disobeying commands.

- **Walking through a crowd:** Your dog should be able to stay under control while walking in a public place with other people around.
- **Sitting and lying down:** Your Sheltie should act on command and remain in place until the evaluator instructs you to release him.
- **Coming when called:** This test determines if your dog will obediently come when called.
- **Reaction to other dogs:** Your dog will be tested on how he reacts to his peers. Grading will depend on his ability to remain calm and in control when other dogs are brought around.
- **Reaction to distractions:** Your dog must not be easily distracted by passing bicycles, joggers, or sudden noises.
- **Supervised separation:** Your dog must be left alone with a stranger without becoming distraught.

Obedience Trials

Shelties can perform very well in the obedience ring. There are three levels of training in which a dog can compete for an obedience title: Novice, Open, and Utility. These trials are open to all registered dogs over the age of six months that are qualified, by training, to participate.

- Novice class dogs usually have had at least one year of work in following practical commands used in everyday living such as *"Heel"* (both with and without a leash), *"Come,"* and *"Stay."*
- Open level is more stringent and includes exercises such as retrieving and jumping hurdles.
- Utility level is the class for the best of the best and includes scent discrimination and silent signaling.

The AKC also has non-title classes that the beginning obedience handler and dog can enter to prepare for the titled ones. Most competitors started by taking obedience classes as a way of gaining control over their pets but found that working with their dogs could be a very rewarding experience. If you are interested in finding out more, a list of scheduled events as well as a copy of the AKC Obedience Regulations is available from the AKC.

Agility Trials

Agility competitions have become more and more popular each year, and the Sheltie has proven to be a breed that excels in these events. It is truly a sport for those energetic owners who want to have fun with their Shelties. Not only will it help create a lasting bond between dog and trainer, but it will also help keep you both fit. In agility trials both the dog and handler need to run at full speed while performing exercises both accurately and safely. Dogs can compete in either the AKC Standard Class, which includes obstacles such as climbing, descending, the A-frame, traversing an elevated dog walk, and crossing a seesaw; or the AKC Jumpers with Weaves Class, which involves jumps, tunnels, and weave poles. Both classes offer increasing levels of difficulty as the dogs compete to earn a Novice, Open, Excellent, or Master title.

For those who have never seen an agility competition, I strongly urge you to attend one in your area, as the excitement that the top dog/handler teams can generate is unparalleled in the competition ring.

Herding Trials

Herding competitions are designed for all herding dog breeds. These competitions are sometimes referred to as "sheepdog trials."

In herding competitions the dogs must move sheep around a field, fences, gates, or enclosures as directed by their handlers. Some farmers use these competitions to teach their dogs proper herding techniques for use on the farm, while other dogs competing are just doing so as a hobby. Regardless, herding trials can provide exercise for the dog. Herding competitions are gaining popularity and are sometimes included as part of agility competitions for herding breeds. The judge looks for the dog's ability to move and control livestock by "fetching," which is bringing the flock to the handler, or "driving," which is moving a flock forward away from the handler. If you are interested in finding out more, a list of scheduled events as well as a copy of the AKC Herding Trial Regulations is available from the AKC.

Other Events to Consider

There has been a recent increase in the popularity of a variety of other events and competitions that you may want to consider participating in with your Sheltie. These include frisbee, flyball, and freestyle dance competitions. These types of events are not limited by size, and the competitions are always designed to be fair to all of the participants. While they are not AKC-sanctioned, they offer a chance for casual dog owners and their energetic pets to get out and socialize (not to mention compete), and they also allow pets to get some extra exercise. If you find that your dog has an abundance of energy that he needs to burn off, I strongly suggest you look into these types of competitions. You can learn about these types of events and if they are held in your area on the Internet.

HOW–TO: HOUSETRAINING

Housetraining a puppy has never been considered a lot of fun for the dog owner. Certain methods, however, can speed up the process.

Paper Training

The objective of paper training is to get your puppy to urinate and defecate on newspapers spread out in an area of your choosing. Naturally, you should choose an area that is easy to clean such as a kitchen or bathroom. Make sure that the area you choose is not too close to your puppy's eating or sleeping areas. Your Sheltie will instinctively try to keep those areas clean and will not excrete near them.

Start by confining your puppy to the area you have chosen until he voids. If he used the paper, remove the top soiled sheet, and place fresh, clean papers under what were formerly the bottom sheets. By doing this, you will be leaving the scent from the bottom papers exposed so that the puppy can relocate the area to repeat the act.

If the puppy misses the paper on his first attempt, get the scent of the dog's urine onto a sheet of newspaper and place it on top of the other sheets. Then thoroughly clean the area where the accident occurred. Removing all scent from the inappropriate area is important so the Sheltie will not become confused by finding his scent in two different locations the next time he has to relieve himself.

Try to remember that after eating, drinking, playing, or waking up, your puppy will probably need to empty his bladder and bowels. Young puppies need to relieve themselves every few hours. Oftentimes the only sign your puppy will give you is that he will begin sniffing the ground, searching for the right place to do his duty. Pick up the puppy, and place him onto the newspaper in the designated area of your home. You can then gently restrain the puppy's movements until he has relieved himself on the paper. Be sure to praise your puppy after he has used the paper.

Crate Training

Crate training offers a faster and easier alternative to paper training. It takes advantage of your puppy's instincts to keep his sleeping area clean. If your puppy is wary on his first encounter with the crate, make the crate more appealing by placing some toys inside. After you confine the puppy to his crate a few times with its excreta, he will quickly learn to restrain himself until you let him out of his crate. Naturally, you must take the puppy outdoors to relieve himself as soon as you let him out of the crate. Establish a time schedule for letting the Sheltie out to relieve himself. As your puppy

becomes more used to the schedule, you can let him out of his crate for longer periods of time. Eventually, you will be able to leave the crate door open at all times without fear of accidents.

Using a crate has additional benefits. A crate is a secure place, where a dog will prefer to sleep, as well as a housetraining aid and traveling crate.

The crate can also serve as an invaluable training tool. If your puppy refuses to listen to your commands, you can pick him up and put him into his crate. When your Sheltie becomes involuntarily separated from his family, he will quickly learn that you are not happy with his performance.

Outdoor Training

Outdoor training begins when your first bring your puppy home. Before taking him indoors, take him for a walk in the area where you want him to eliminate. Give your puppy plenty of time to do his duty, and be sure to praise him for a job well done. Verbal praise and petting will help build your puppy's confidence and will increase your chances of future successful performances.

Most puppies need to relieve themselves as many as six times a day, so you will need to take your puppy outdoors about once every three to four hours. Walking the puppy after each of his meals is also advisable. A puppy's stomach will exert additional pressure on the bladder, so do not wait too long. You should take your puppy for his last walk as late in the evening as possible so that your Sheltie puppy is less likely to have accidents during the night. If you continue to bring your puppy to the same area each time, he will eventually seek out this area on its own.

Cleaning Up

While canine droppings are aesthetically unpleasant, it is your responsibility to clean up the mess. Many towns and cities have made it illegal *not* to clean up after your pet.

Wherever you walk your Sheltie, carry a plastic bag or pooper scooper with you. Dispose of the mess in its proper place. When cleaning your garden or yard, pick up and dispose of the droppings in well-sealed plastic bags in a sealed garbage can. For accidents that happen in the home, clean with an odor-eliminating disinfectant. Do not use ammonia because the smell may remind your puppy of his urine.

Accidents Will Happen

If you discover that while you slept, your Sheltie puppy could no longer control himself, remember that this *was an accident*. Getting angry or administering punishment will not do you or your puppy any good. Puppies have very short memories. If you do not catch your puppy in the act or make the discovery shortly afterward, a scolding will only confuse your pet.

Kennel Clubs and Organizations

The American Kennel Club (AKC)
260 Madison Avenue
New York, NY 10016
Web site: *www.akc.org*

The American Shetland Sheepdog Association
(ASSA)
Krystn Messer, Corresponding Secretary
80 Doe Court
Apex, NC 27523-8400
Web site: *www.assa.org*
E-mail: *assamail@echowyn.com*

Orthopedic Foundation for Animals
2300 E. Nifong Boulevard
Columbia, MO 65201-3806
Web site: *www.offa.org*

Canine Eye Registration Foundation
South Campus Court, Building C
Purdue University
West Lafayette, IN 47907
Web site: *www.vmdb.org/cerf.html*

The American Veterinary Medical Association
1931 North Meacham Road, Suite 100
Schaumburg, IL 60173-4360
Web site: *www.avma.org*

Magazines

Dog Fancy
P.O. Box 6050
Mission Viejo, CA 92690
Web site: *www.dogchannel.com/dog-magazines/
dogfancy/default.aspx*

Dogs Monthly
61 Great Whyte,
Ramsey, Huntingdon, PE26 1HJ UK
Web site: *http://www.dogsmonthly.co.uk*

Useful Literature

Eldridge, Debra M., Carlson, Liisa D., Carlson, Delbert G., and James M. Giffin. *Dog Owner's Home Veterinary Handbook,* Fourth Edition. New York, NY: Howell Book House, 1997.

Forsyth, Robert. *Forsyth Guide to Successful Dog Showing.* New York, NY: Howell Book House, 1975.

Fox, Michael W. *Dog Body Dog Mind: Exploring Canine Consciousness and Total Well-Being.* Guilford, CT: The Lyons Press, 2007.

Kalstone, Shirlee. *How to Housebreak Your Dog in 7 Days.* New York, NY: Bantam Books, 2004.

McGowan, Charlotte Clem. *The Shetland Sheepdog in America.* Crawford, CO: Alpine Publications, Inc., 1999.

McKinney, Betty Jo and Barbara Reiseberg. *Sheltie Talk.* Crawford CO: Alpine Publications, Inc., 1985.

Millan, Cesar and Melissa Jo Peltier. *Be the Pack Leader: Use Ceasar's Way to Transform Your Life ... And Your Dog.* New York, NY: Three Rivers Press, 2008.

Riddle, Maxwell. *The New Complete Shetland Sheepdog.* New York, NY: Howell Book House, 1991.

Schwartz, Charlotte. *Shetland Sheepdog: A Comprehensive Guide to Owning and Caring for Your Dog.* Allenhurst, NJ: Kennel Club Books, Inc., 2003.

I N D E X

061096

About the Author

Jaime J. Sucher is Director of Research and Development for a manufacturer of pet products. He is the author of *Golden Retrievers* and *Shih Tzus*, and has written numerous articles on pet nutrition.

Important Note

This pet owner's manual tells the reader how to buy or adopt and care for a Shetland Sheepdog. The author and publisher consider it important to point out that the advice given in this book is meant primarily for normally developed dogs of excellent physical health and good character.

Anyone who adopts a fully grown dog should be aware that the animal has already formed his basic impressions of humans. The new owner should watch the dog carefully, including his behavior toward humans, and should meet the previous owner.

Caution is further advised in the association of children with dogs, in meeting with other dogs, and in exercising the dog without proper safeguards.

Even well-behaved and carefully supervised dogs sometimes do damage to someone else's property or cause accidents. It is therefore in the owner's interest to be adequately insured against such eventualities, and we strongly urge all dog owners to purchase a liability policy that covers their dog(s).

Cover Photos

Shutterstock: front cover, back cover, inside front cover, inside back cover.

Photo Credits

Gerry Bucsis/Barbara Somerville: pages 4, 12, 22, 23, 24, 65, 68; Seth Casteel: pages 18, 27, 47, 81; Kent Dannen: pages 6, 89; Cheryl Ertelt: pages 9, 34, 36, 38, 46; Sharon Eide Elizabeth Flynn: pages 5, 63, 66; jeanmfogle.com: pages 11, 22, 28, 39, 45, 64, 82, 87; Paulette Johnson: pages 10, 13, 20, 21, 25, 29, 33, 37, 41, 42, 43, 44, 48, 50, 55, 57, 90, 91, 93; Liz Kaye: pages 14, 52, 67; Shutterstock: pages 2–3, 17, 26, 32, 40, 71, 72, 78, 85; Connie Summers/Paulette Johnson: page 60; Steve Surfman: pages 74, 75, 77.

All inquiries should be addressed to:
Barron's Educational Series, Inc.
250 Wireless Boulevard
Hauppauge, NY 11788
www.barronseduc.com

Library of Congress Catalog Card No. 2010933387

ISBN: 978-0-7641-4590-2

Printed in China
9 8 7 6 5 4 3 2 1